STRANGER AT THE GATES

STRANGER
at the GATES

A Summer in Mississippi

by

TRACY SUGARMAN

Illustrated by the Author

New Foreword
by Charles McLaurin
Foreword
by Fannie Lou Hamer
Introduction
by Congressman John Lewis

PROSPECTA PRESS

To June, who made it all happen.

CONTENTS

NEW FOREWORD

During the summer of 1964 more than a thousand college students from across this country converged upon the state of Mississippi as part of the Freedom Summer Project. Mostly young, white, middle-class kids, they spent the summer in the homes of poor sharecroppers and other laborers. They were answering a call from the Student Nonviolent Coordinating Committee (SNCC) for volunteers to spend a summer helping the black population in a racially oppressive Mississippi gain their freedom by registering to vote and attending Freedom Schools.

In 1964, blacks made up nearly 40 percent of the total state population, yet only approximately 5 percent were registered to vote—and only a few of that number even dared to show up at a polling place on election day. Voting was not a privilege granted to blacks but an action that, if practiced, invoked a fear of reprisals that could have meant death to an individual or a group.

The young came in sandals, with pens, pencils, and a willing spirit to correct a political wrong: a blatant history of injustice against a segmented group of people. When the group arrived in Mississippi in June, three civil rights volunteers in Neshoba County were already missing, presumed victims of the Ku Klux Klan, who were bent on keeping things the way they were at all costs—usually through violence. When, after several weeks, the worst was confirmed—the three young civil rights volunteers were dead—the movement was not deterred. Instead, it picked up momentum.

Those three disappearances and then confirmed deaths brought national media attention to the plight of black Mississippians. Not only were voting rights severely compromised, but there was not one black elected official at the state level or in any of Mississippi's eighty-two counties except for the all-black town of Mound Bayou.

The young volunteers of the Freedom Summer Project played a key role in assisting black Mississippians to organize the Mississippi Freedom Democratic Party (MFDP). MFDP, a parallel party to the Mississippi Democratic Party, planned to challenge the regular all-white Mississippi delegation to the Democratic National Convention—a challenge based on the fact that the black population was being denied participation in the political process at local precincts in the selection of delegates to the county, district, and state conventions.

SNCC organizers had helped black citizens set up the political process for the MFDP across the state, and on April 6, 1964, MFDP held its state convention in the Masonic Temple in Jackson, Mississippi. During the convention—where the influential activist Ella Baker was the speaker—sixty-eight delegates were selected to attend the Democratic National Convention in Atlantic City, New Jersey, to claim their right to be seated.

The first step in the MFDP seating challenge process was a hearing before the National Democratic Party Credentials Committee. Although there were testimonies by Aaron E. Henry of the MFDP and by national civil rights leader Dr. Martin Luther King Jr., the testimony that mattered most came from a sharecropper, Fannie Lou Hamer. In a resonant voice, Hamer told the committee about her eviction from her plantation home after she made an application to register to vote in Sunflower County. Hamer captured the full attention of the members of the Credentials Committee and of the national TV audience when she went on to describe the brutal beating she suffered in 1963 when she and other activists were falsely accused and thrown into a Montgomery County jail.

So damaging was Fannie Lou Hamer's testimony that President Lyndon B. Johnson called a press conference, hoping to get her off TV. When the evening news insisted on carrying the full Hamer testimony, a furious President Johnson sent his potential vice-president, Hubert H. Humphrey, to offer the MFDP a compromise giving them two seats "at large." Regarded by the MFDP as "nothing" because it would change "nothing" in Mississippi for the black population, the offer was unanimously rejected by the delegates. The regular all-white Mississippi delegation was asked to pledge its support to the National Democratic Party ticket, but the delegation refused and went home. In its absence the MFDP delegates began filling the vacant convention seats under the Mississippi banner. Meanwhile, President Johnson, worried that a floor fight could cost him support of the southern wing of the Democratic Party, arranged to have the convention nominate him by acclimation, and no delegate vote on the convention floor was taken,

While the MFDP did not succeed in unseating the regular Mississippi Democratic Party delegation in Atlantic City in 1964, the challenge again attracted national media attention to the shameful conditions under which the state of Mississippi was forcing its black population to live. In addition, the National Democratic Party pledged not to seat a segregated state delegation in the future. In the 1964 presidential election, Mississippi and the rest of the Deep South went Republican. This was just the tip of the iceberg.

Many of the successes of that hot summer of 1964 were thanks to the volunteers who spent the summer living in crowded and stifling homes with outside toilets, and who walked endless miles on unpaved roads, daily facing fear and danger in an attempt to register black voters with the MFDP and begin to correct the atrocity of inequality.

Fifty years later, we should welcome the reprinting of Tracy Sugarman's memoir, *Stranger at the Gates*. Sugarman, a writer and illustrator who died in 2013, was a lifelong activist and a friend of Fannie Lou Hamer. He joined the students as a volunteer in Mississippi—not only participating but observing, taking notes, and making his wonderful drawings. His book is a vivid, on-the-spot account of a time when lives were lost, lives were changed, and the word *freedom* took on a new meaning.

Charles McLaurin
Indianola, Mississippi, 2014

FOREWORD

Ninety percent of the Negro people in Mississippi have gone to church all their lives. They have lived with the hope that if they kept "standing up" in a Christian manner, things would change. After we found out that Christian love alone wouldn't cure the sickness in Mississippi, then we knew we had other things to do.

There was no real Civil Rights Movement in the Negro community in Mississippi before the 1964 Summer Project. There were people that wanted change, but they hadn't dared to come out and try to do something, to try to change the way things were. But after the 1964 project when all of the young people came down for the summer—an exciting and remarkable summer—Negro people in the Delta began moving. People who had never before tried, though they had always been anxious to do something, began moving. Now, in 1966, even Negroes who live on the plantations slip off the plantations and go to civil rights meetings. "We wanted to do this so long," they say. When some of us get up and blast out at the meetings, these women go back home—these men go back home—and in the next day or two the kids come. They say, "My mother told us what you talked about last night." That's great! To see kids, to see these people—to see how far they've come since 1964! To me it's one of the greatest things that ever happened in Mississippi. And it's a direct result of the Summer Project in 1964.

I believe in Christianity. To me, the 1964 Summer Project was the beginning of a New Kingdom right here on earth. The kinds of people who came down from the North—from all over—who didn't know anything about us—were like the Good Samaritan. In that Bible story, the people had passed by the wounded man—like the church has passed the Negroes in Mississippi—and never taken the time to see what was going on. But these people who came to Mississippi that summer—although they were strangers—walked up to our door. They started something that no one could ever stop. These people were willing to move in a nonviolent way to bring a change in the South. Although they were strangers, they were the best friends we ever met. This was the beginning of the New Kingdom in Mississippi. To me, if I had to choose today between the church and these young people—and I was brought up in the church and I'm not against the church—I'd choose these young people. They did something in Mississippi that gave us the hope that we had prayed for for so many years. We had wondered if there was anybody human enough to see us as human beings instead of animals.

These young people were so Christlike! James Chaney, Andrew Goodman, and Michael Schwerner gave their lives that one day we would be free. If Christ were here today, He would be just like these young people who the southerners called radicals and beatniks. Christ was called a Beelzebub, called so many names. But He was Christ. I can hardly express what those students and that summer meant to me—what it meant to the people who didn't dare say anything. Because when they would get a chance, they would express how they felt. As a result of that summer, we Negroes are working—slow—but we're moving. Not only did it have an effect on the black people of Mississippi but it touched some of the white people who don't yet dare speak out. This is important.

My family was like thousands of other families in Mississippi. My grandmother was a slave. My mother passed away in 1961. She was ninety-eight years old. We were taught something in Mississippi I'm not ashamed of today. We were taught to love. We were taught to not hate. And we were taught to stand on principle, stand on what we believe. I often remember my mother telling me, "If you respect yourself, one day somebody else will respect you."

The reason that we Negroes in Mississippi are not bitter is because most of us were brought up in church from an early age. A child has to be taught to hate. We were taught to love and to have faith. My father used to read a scripture from the Bible: "Faith is the substance of things hoped for and the evidence of things not seen." We Negroes had hoped and we had faith to hope, though we didn't know what we had hoped for. When the people came to Mississippi in 1964, to us it was the result of all our faith—all we had always hoped for. Our prayers and all we had lived for day after day hadn't been in vain. In 1964 the faith that we had hoped for started to be translated into action. Now we have action, and we're doing something that will not only free the black man in Mississippi but hopefully will free the white one as well. No man is an island to himself.

I used to say when I was working so hard in the fields, if I could go to Washington—to the Justice Department—to the FBI—get close enough to let them know what was going on in Mississippi, I was sure that things would change in a week. Now that I have traveled across America, been to the Congress, to the Justice Department, to the FBI, I am faced with things I'm not too sure I wanted to find out. The sickness in Mississippi is not a Mississippi sickness. This is America's sickness. We talk about democracy, we talk about the land of the free, but it's not true. We talk about freedom of speech, but in every corner of this United States men who try to speak the truth are crushed. The crisis in Mississippi made young people who are going to the college campuses all across the United States start to question: "What is going on around here?" Now, because of these young people, we have a chance to make democracy a reality. We often talk about it. We often express it. But you can go to the slums in Harlem, the slums in Chicago, the slums in California, the slums in Pennsylvania, the slums in Washington, D.C., and you'll find the race problem no different in kind from the problem in Mississippi. We don't have democracy now. But the great part about the young people in this country is that they want to change things. They want to make democracy a reality in the whole country—if it is not already too late.

Mrs. Fannie Lou Hamer
Ruleville, Mississippi, 1966

PREFACE

As if released by the shattering frenzy of the struggle, gusting winds of change raced through the postwar years. They altered the face of Africa and Asia and buffeted a Europe that was struggling to stand. The death of fascism heralded a new beginning. A surging tide of expectation touched the disinherited everywhere. In America, the Negro, who had been waiting a hundred years for the death of "Jim Crow," shuffled his G.I. boots impatiently and stared hard at his democratic society.

From the moment the U.S. Supreme Court declared in 1954 that "separate but equal" schools were unconstitutional, the American Negro launched a sustained assault on discrimination and segregation. Adapting the Gandhian tactic of nonviolence, he challenged his society with his cry of "Freedom Now!" One hundred years after Appomattox, his "sit-ins" and "Freedom Rides," "wade-ins" and "kneel-ins" were defying the legal evasions and moral pretensions of America. Against police dogs and fire hoses, vigilante shotguns and torches, he placed his body in eloquent testimony to his belief in Christianity and the United States Constitution.

Like so many others in the United States, I was moved by this sacrifice and appalled that in this land it should be necessary. From the moment I returned from Normandy and left the U.S. Navy in 1945, I had worked as an illustrator. Whenever possible, I had sought out the reportorial assignment. Whether in "cracking plants" or aseptic laboratories, assembly lines or amid the dusty roar of construction, I had toted my sketchbook, recording the face of postwar America. The mounting urgency of the racial crisis became for me and my wife a crisis of conscience as well. In some way we knew we must do what we could to help. Even as President Kennedy urged a sluggish Congress to enact relief for the Negro American through the Civil Rights Act of 1964, the Civil Rights Movement was preparing an attack on the most inviolable fortress of segregation in the United States. Against the Klan, the White Citizens Councils, and the might of a hostile society's police, a thousand unarmed students prepared to move into Mississippi. They were to receive their orientation at the Western College for Women in Oxford, Ohio.

In family council, we decided that this could be our way to help. June would maintain our home base with our children, raising funds and building support for the Mississippi Summer Project. And I would accompany the students to Mississippi, recording their "Odyssey" for the country to see. Pamela Illot of CBS News assured me that she would use my pictures and tapes. The result was her lovely half-hour television documentary, "How Beautiful on the Mountains," that appeared on her series, "Lamp Unto My Feet." In Washington the U.S.I.A. magazine, *Al Hayat*, promised to use my drawings and my notes to tell the civil rights story overseas. I left for Oxford feeling that there would be an audience for the pictures I wanted to draw. In the months following that long summer, the drawings helped carry the implications of the struggle in magazines sent by the U.S. to India, Africa, and Europe. At home they appeared in newspapers, magazines, and in exhibitions on many campuses and in many cities.

No one who went to Mississippi in 1964 returned the same. Some were disoriented, some embittered, some exalted by a new vision of America. I came home from the dusty roads of the Delta with a deeper understanding of patriotism, an unshakeable respect for commitment, and an abiding belief in the power of love.

T.S.

Westport, Connecticut
April, 1966

INTRODUCTION

The first time I ever traveled to Mississippi was on the Freedom Rides. I was one of the 13 original riders who left Washington, DC on May 4, 1961, to test a recent Supreme Court decision that desegregated interstate bus travel. Our goal was to ride from Washington, D.C. to New Orleans in an integrated fashion, through the Deep South, where it was illegal for black and white passengers to sit next to each other.

Because of mob violence some of us encountered in South Carolina and cities in Alabama, the rides were almost suspended. But we believed we had to continue because if we allowed brutality to deter us, then it would send a message that violence could silence a non-violent campaign. We were determined to carry on, despite the threat to our lives. We continued on until we got to Jackson, Mississippi.

We were immediately taken to jail, but busloads of peaceful protestors kept coming until we filled the city and county jails. Eventually we were transferred to a notorious prison farm named Parchmen Penitentiary, a 21,000 acre farm owned by the state and worked by inmates. We stayed in Parchmen for more than three weeks. They had tried to break us there, but when we emerged, we were more convinced than ever before that we could take on the challenge of voting rights in Mississippi.

It was very dangerous to be a civil rights worker in Mississippi in the mid-sixties.SNCC's files revealed that since work in 1961 began, there had been over 150 incidents of violence perpetrated against civil rights workers. Several had been killed, but only five percent of the voting- age African Americans had been registered, still the lowest in the nation.

We knew that somehow we needed to create a sense of urgency, so SNCC's Mississippi leader, a brilliant man named Robert Moses, suggested we invite people to come to see the resistance in Mississippi for themselves. My role as chairman of SNCC, during those days, was to travel around the country to college campuses and ask students to come. Hundreds came to Mississippi that summer, and Tracy Sugarman was one of them.

This book is his account of his experiences there at a revolutionary period in American history. The students who came during that summer helped to make a shift in American politics. Mississippi became the best organized SNCC effort in the country, and the foundation that Robert Moses laid to carry out a mock election, called Freedom Vote, and then to establish the Mississippi Freedom Democratic Party, with Fannie Lou Hamer at the helm, changed the shape of Democratic Party politics. It also created a network of political activists who are still working for change there today. That is why, even with all the problems that remain, Mississippi still has the highest number of black elected officials of any state in the country.

Tracy Sugarman's story is important because it tells the story of how this happened. We are very fortunate today that most of us do not have to fear for our lives to register and vote, but there was a time, not so long ago, when people had to give their lives so that you and I could participate more freely in the democratic process. The right to vote is precious, almost sacred. It is the most powerful non-violent tool we have for change in a democratic society. And this is the story of what one man saw, and what was sacrificed to secure that right for all American citizens.

Congressman John Lewis
April, 2014

Part I

TRAINING

1

The Western College for Women, in Oxford, Ohio, was dreaming in moonlight as I turned off the state highway and wound up the gentle rise to the Administration building. The summer holiday had begun, and the campus slept undisturbed. Single lights in janitors' basements made pale carpets on the deserted green. I parked the Chevvy and rested against the steering wheel, breathing the cool damp of Ohio farmland. A dozen kids lounged on the grass, silhouetted against the brightness of the deep windows. A girl's voice rose sweet and quiet as a guitar gently added to the fuzzy complaint of the cicadas. "Good news is a-comin'—good news." I moved up the walk past them, feeling their eyes on my cotton and Dacron suit and the skinny-brimmed Madison Avenue straw hat. "Newspaper man," somebody grunted, and the guitar changed again. I paused at the lighted door, held by the young voices, the moonlight, the smell of the new-cut lawn. "Hush little baby, don't say a word. Mama's gonna buy you a mockin' bird. If that mockin' bird don't sing…"

I thought of our two-year-old crawling into our bed between us, sixteen years before, and June singing softly in the dark, Dickie cradled in the crook of her arm.

"If that mockin' bird don't sing, Mama's gonna buy you a diamon' ring."

In the lounge the kids were talking earnestly in small groups, asking questions, sorting the literature in the folders they'd been given, a few looking shy and hanging back. The Negro kids were the cool ones

("They're Snick staff, and man, they know"). The volunteers were the questioners, trying hard to relate, questioning the staff, seeking the "word," asking, asking.

"But how could you…."

"But why did you…."

"How do they dare…."

The appraising, watchful, cautious, brown faces—being careful.

"Now look, man, this is the way it is…."

"Yeah, but Smith ain't Mississippi…."

The khaki pants, the desert boots, the open Brooks Brothers shirt, the denim skirts, the bright blouse, the sandals, the bright eyes, the horn-rimmed glasses, the pocket books of poetry, Jung, Salinger, *The Trojan Wars, Winnie-the-Pooh, Mad Magazine* and *The New Republic*, the easy grace and quick laughter of America's children of higher education. And the questioning, and the sober reflective look that said "I understand."

The platoon leaders were Negro boys and girls, from Mississippi. They wore denim jackets and work shirts, and they were studying their troops. They played it cool, but they looked tired.

I moved through the lounge and into the large side room marked "Registration." A staff meeting of the Council of Churches leaders was being held at its far end. Bruce Hanson caught my eye, smiled, and rose to greet me. He looked drawn and concerned.

"Sign in," he said. "You're Press."

The weary girl at the desk filled out a yellow tag and pinned it on my jacket. I moved to the door and pushed out into the soft darkness of the campus.

The singers were standing now, clustered in a tight knot at the end of the walk. The voices swelled as I moved to join them. Two moved apart to let me in, and my voice lifted with theirs.

"Deep in my heart I know that I do believe." My eyes burned and I was glad of the darkness. I unpinned the press badge and slid it into my pocket.

I lay on the bed and regarded the suitcase which leaned against the opposite bed. A crumpled seersucker jacket had been tossed on the bed, and an empty sleeve lay negligently hanging across the battered leather of the case. I wondered what my roommate would be like. The boy that came in was pale, a little soft in the middle, I thought. His dark hair was damp and long. It kept drifting down toward his eyes, which were deep-set and seemed black in the cold light of the overhead bulb. He brushed the curly hair back indifferently and stopped as the door closed behind him. I swung my legs off the bed and stood up. He took my hand quietly as I introduced myself. His voice was soft and southern.

"Now look, man, this is the way that it is...."

"I'm John Strickland."

The grin was gentle and brief. An air of melancholy moved with him, seeming to blunt his movements and dull his responses. Only once in the days ahead was I to glimpse the bright intelligence and banked passion that glowed inside. But usually our conversations were brief, and I sensed a reticence in the boy that I preferred to honor. Nevertheless, by the week's end, I realized how rare a man was John Strickland. Not only was he a southerner, a white southerner, he was the seventh child of a Savannah sharecropper. To totally disorient my preconceptions of white, southern sharecroppers it was in due course revealed that John was a junior at Harvard! He was here to study "community relations."

"What will you be doing, John?" I asked

He frowned and studied his hands that rested in his lap. "We're supposed to build bridges to the white community in Mississippi."

A wry smile flitted across his face. "If they're like my daddy, it's going to be tough. Real tough."

Two weeks before the orientation began in Oxford, Ohio, Charles McLaurin was beaten by the Mississippi Highway Patrol. In all the arrests, the endless days and weeks of outlasting time in Ruleville, Greenville, Greenwood, never had he been hit. The afternoon I had met him in 1963 when he was visiting in Connecticut he had joked about it. "Not me! I'm lucky, man!"

But the Highway Patrol had beaten him now. The SNCC staff workers had been forced off the road by the Patrol as they headed for headquarters in Atlanta. They had beaten the driver and then herded the five young men to jail. The Patrol had known they were heading east on the highway, and they had simply mousetrapped them. There was no charge, just arrest, "held for investigation." One month later Andy Goodman, Mickey Schwerner, and James Chaney would be arrested, "held for investigation," released at night, and killed.

One by one the five Negroes were summoned from the cell. McLaurin was the last. From his cell he could hear the murmur of the interrogation, the angry shouting, the numbing sound of flesh striking flesh, the surprised gasps of pain. In an agony of terror he watched his body, unbidden, move from the open cell. "I watched myself go," he says. "It was like it was happening to somebody else. I watched my feet move, one after the other till I reached the top of the iron stairs."

"We're gonna light a lamp in Ruleville, and it's gonna shine all over that Delta." Charles McLaurin, SNCC.

"Down here, boy!"

He remembers looking down, the two policemen looking ridiculously tiny, their white faces turned up to McLaurin. Suddenly he was standing at the bottom of the stairs and the two police faces filled the room.

"Boy," said the patrolman, in a conversational voice, "are you a Negro or a nigger?"

McLaurin swallowed, his throat tight and parched.

"I'm a Negro."

The patrolman slammed the back of his fist into McLaurin's mouth, splitting his lip. Tears betrayed the pain, and his mouth was full of blood.

"Boy," repeated the patrolman, his voice level and quiet, "are you a Negro or a nigger?"

McLaurin looked straight at the man.

"I'm a Negro."

The patrolman at his side jolted him with a straight punch that exploded on the side of his jaw, pitching him in a thudding sprawl on the concrete.

"I felt no pain," he says, "but my back teeth felt loose, and my mouth was a mess. As I lay there at the bottom of the stairs I knew they would keep hitting me until they killed me if I didn't say 'nigger.' That man had to hear me say it. He just had to. I got up and he said, 'Boy, are you a Negro or a nigger?' And I said, 'I'm a nigger.' He nodded, and I left the jail."

The second day at Oxford I found McLaurin conducting a workshop on Sunflower County. He tilted back in his chair and the opaque sunglasses moved slowly across the faces straining forward to hear. "Sunflower County is in the heart of the Mississippi Delta. This is the home of Senator James Eastland. His bank is in Ruleville, and his office is over the bank. Indianola is the county seat, and it's the home of the White Citizens Council. We're gonna start in Ruleville, because those folks will stand up. And we're gonna change Sunflower County. We're gonna light a lamp in Ruleville, and it's gonna shine all over that Delta." I looked at the yellow chalk map that he had sketched on the blackboard—Drew, Ruleville,

Cleveland, Shaw, Indianola, Sunflower and Bolivar counties. A long arrow stretched from little Ruleville at the top of the county to Indianola at the bottom. "Twenty-five miles" was lettered on the arrow. McLaurin grinned as I shook hands with him at the end of the session.

"Good to see you again," he said.

"Mac, I'd like to go with your group for the summer. I want to show people what you're doing. Can you use an artist?"

The eyes behind the dark glasses were still, and then he nodded several times. "Hell, yes." He grinned. "Glad to have you."

Jack Preiss paused next to me on the soft tar road in front of the Administration building. He squinted in the brightness and absently watched the students sweat and yell, chasing a volleyball that was being used for a soccer scrimmage. A pick-up game had started, and the tension of the past two days was exploding in the grunts of body contact as they checked and slammed. The too-light ball would soar like a demented bird, and the sweat-drenched bodies would chase it, laughter spilling behind them.

"It's not working," he said.

We moved across the road and under a huge beech tree. The sounds of the scrimmage were less strident, and we stretched out on the shaded lawn. Preiss wrinkled his forehead and rubbed his freckled fish back and forth against the fleshy tip of his nose.

"It's really not working. I've been listening for two and a half days, and they're really not getting through to each other. I'm worried. They don't have a hell of a lot of time."

He sat up and wrapped his arms around his knees. His eyes moved in pursuit as the kids ran stumbling after the ball.

"It's Tuesday, and they leave for Mississippi on Sunday. They're all talking about it, but they're not listening."

Reverend Bruce Hanson, National Council of Churches of Christ, COFO co-ordinator.

I had met Preiss in the dining room the first night. He was a sandy-complexioned, middle-sized man. Reddish hair edged back from his forehead, betraying his forty years, for his crinkling smile and freckled face made him seem boyish. He was a comfortable man to be with. The night before we had sat late over beers, swapping war stories and speculating about the weeks that stretched ahead. His job was to work with the group dynamics of the orientation week, and he was struggling to establish some real communication between the two groups that stubbornly refused to flow.

You watched the kids listening, and you knew they were wondering, "Am I good enough?"

"They don't really know how they feel yet," he said. "Maybe the play-acting will do it tomorrow. Something better had!" He kicked at a small ant hill with the heel of his sneaker.

"Christ, a week's just not enough time. They've got to get to know each other."

For two days the lectures and workshops had been mounting an unrelenting assault on the volunteers. I wondered uneasily if this perhaps was not the real screening process. We were being frightened, and I sensed that this was a calculated process; a sharp, scalpeled insertion of reality intended to kill or cure. The terror and violence of Mississippi was detailed and dissected. The extents of police brutality were catalogued, and the unreal world of the barbarous newsreel and the tabloid spread was suddenly becoming our world. The volunteers listened to the incredible stories of beatings and murder and knew surely and profoundly that this incredible world was credible. The knowledge served only to widen the immensity of the gulf that stretched between them and the field workers.

The cool self-sufficiency of those SNCC people reminded me of the RAF veterans of the Battle of Britain. We had come fresh and eager from the States, trained, primed, and itching to find the war and win it. These tired, old-young men had regarded us politely, nodded, and returned to the private society of those who knew because they had shared it together. No insult had been intended. They were glad we were there to win the war. It had simply ceased to be the same war they had fought. We had so envied the knowing grace of them. Each who was left had been tested, purified of the doubts that nagged us in our Quonset huts. And they regarded us as brash, pampered youngsters, overpaid, overtrained, and overequipped. They deeply envied us our pay, our training, and our equipment. We were never to really know their world, for they were to pack their neat duffles, step quickly back, and move swiftly into the backwash of a war that had moved on. How could we know the pain and the nightmares that were packed in those duffles? But here the pain and the nightmares were being exhibited like ghoulish displays. There seemed to be a muffled drumbeat you sensed in those first days of that curious week at

Oxford. "They've *got* to know. They've *got* to know." For we were moving into the same battle as these quick, knowing field workers. You watched the kids listening, and you knew they were wondering, "Am I good enough?"

My God, what if you really were beaten. What if they held you and smashed you. Could you take it—really take it—and not cut and run? The SNCC kid this afternoon had said, "You've got to expect to be scared." Okay. Think about it. What really frightened you? The dogs, maybe. Those terrible pictures of dogs biting children in Birmingham. You tried to imagine being bitten, being smashed. Try as you might you couldn't imagine being killed. Not really. Three hours before, in this auditorium, Ed King had stood and tried to tell you what it was like. One side of his face was dreadfully scared by the Mississippi vigilantes who had tried to kill him.

"Trust your instinct," he said. "When that feeling in the pit of your stomach says 'Duck!' or 'Run!' trust it. It may save your life. It saved mine."

"Save your life!" Even the words sounded theatrical. *Come on, man. Don't put me on.* But they watched the late afternoon sun touch King's livid cheek and knew it was so.

2

My eyes moved around the crowded hall, watching the students settling into the wooden theatre seats. How many had left, I wondered, after the session with King this afternoon. Maybe while we ate our dinner boys had tossed dirty sweat socks into duffles and made their way quietly to the Greyhound station in Oxford. And the girls, talking so earnestly into the phones that tied them to home, how many had said, "Maybe you're right, Mom. It's not for me."

If any had left, you couldn't tell. The students bunched in at the doors that flanked the rear of the auditorium and broke into twos and threes as they moved down the aisles and into the rapidly filling rows. The weight of the afternoon heat still lay in the dusty hall, and the windows that opened wide on the still June evening brought no vagrant breeze. The movie screen stood nakedly white on the stage in the yellowish light of the hall. A group of SNCC field workers moved easily through the crowds and found six seats in the first row. Their denim jackets seemed almost a uniform in the room of bright blouses and sport shirts. Their heads would bend toward each other, and one could tell they were laughing by the movement of their shoulders. If they felt the eyes of the room on them, they never acknowledged it.

A small staff group of three stood quietly watching, their backs to the peeling yellow plaster of the wall between the doors. Jim Forman, a bushy-haired, brown bear of a man, was the most imposing. He had spoken to the volunteers on the very first morning, a large-voiced, no-nonsense, practical doer. At thirty, he was Executive Field Secretary of SNCC. The T shirt under the blue overalls looked soiled with sweat, his heavy face glowed with heat, and he stood as if planted, his strong-muscled arms folded across his chest. To his left was John Lewis, National Chairman of SNCC. He seemed small against the bulk of Forman. His hands were lost behind him, resting in the rear pockets of his jeans. His shoulders rested against the wall and his neat bullet head was tipped forward, his chin resting in the V of his open work shirt. Only his eyes moved. They appeared drowsy, seeming to brush slowly around the hall. The heavy lids blinked like the shutters of a camera, dreamily capturing the image, closing, opening once again. His upper lip was heavy, overhanging the lower, and it added to the image of a somnolent beaver.

The first thing you noticed about the third man was the spanking neatness of the blue overalls, the snowy white of the T shirt. His body was compact and slim, and there was at once an air of modesty and dignity about him. His young face was alert and pleasant, and his eyes behind the glasses regarded the world with intelligence and a melancholy gentleness. Bob Moses was the Program Director of the Council of Federated Organizations, a group which had been formed to sponsor the Summer Project in Mississippi. The Southern Christian Leadership Council, the Council on Racial Equality, the Commission on Religion and Race of the National Council of Churches, and his own group, the Student Nonviolent Coordinating Committee, had combined forces to work out the strategy and the logistics for Moses' plan. In the long wretched winter nights in the Delta he had fashioned a scheme so daring that it had frightened even the young field workers with whom he worked. It took weeks of patient reasoning to convince them that this could work. He stood now, a pliant sapling, his feet slightly parted. His face moving quietly, his glasses catching the light, he looked at these youngsters who had heard his forlorn pipe and come running. This unlikeliest Pied Piper, a modest Negro Master of Philosophy from Harvard, looked searchingly about him. His face seemed impassive. If a muscle in his jaw moved or if the crease between his dark brows seemed deeper, one couldn't really say in that badly lit room.

"Don't come to Mississippi this summer to save the Mississippi Negro," he said yesterday. "Only come if you understand, really understand, that his freedom and yours are one."

His voice had been so soft that everyone had leaned forward toward the rostrum. They had heard him before, at Berkeley, at Wesleyan, in New York. Somehow the homely sweetness of this man had caught them and drawn them to Oxford. Now here they were, the white and Negro children come to bear witness from the campuses of America. They leaned forward, and looked hard, for now they sensed the reality of the commitment that he had initiated back at school. He had returned their challenge as he always did. In a calm and quiet voice he had said, "Maybe we're not going to get very many people registered this summer. Maybe, even, we're not going to get very many people into the Freedom Schools. Maybe all we're going to do is live through this summer. In Mississippi, that will be so much!"

Moses had watched them bleed. He had watched them bleed to death. For three cruel years he had clasped hands with death. He loved Herbert Lee and Medgar Evers, and when they were killed he felt altered and lonely. The violence and the pain were scars he would carry privately forever, for they were an obscene offense to his gentle spirit. Of his own arrests and beatings he never spoke, but the savagery heaped daily on the

"Maybe all we're going to do is live through this summer."

head of the Negro in Mississippi moved him to a calculating action which could change the system that fostered it. Those who knew him best said that even more than the revolting fury of the white violence, the boundless, numbing ignorance of the Mississippi Negro simply appalled and overwhelmed him. Everything in this highly complicated twentieth-century man was offended by the crippling ignorance. He knew that this was the white weapon that emasculated and robbed, that made mock of progress and political sloganeering.

The Supreme Court decision of 1954 had not altered anything in Mississippi. Not one white classroom had been integrated by the first frightened Negro child, and the only visible response to the prohibition of "separate but equal" was the hasty building of Negro schools in some communities where no schools had existed at all. Mississippi was determined to keep its Negroes docile and ill educated, for a time-entrenched cotton society was built on the immense base of cheap Negro labor. Moses knew that the only way to break the rigidity of the system was to develop local Negro leadership. Where in this carefully ordered society which conspired to perpetuate itself on every level could he hope to find it? Who could stand against the massed ranks of Mississippi clergy, judiciary, journalists, educators, legislators, employers, and landlords? Who could say "No!" in a voice that would be heard?

The handful of SNCC field workers were tough and endlessly resourceful. For three frustrating years they had fought a guerrilla attack on the apathy and fear that had immobilized the Negro community for a hundred years. The McLaurins, the Cobbs, the Formans had started to kindle the flames that would warm and rouse the sleeping gentle giant. But Moses knew it would take whites from the North to catch the conscience of white America. It would take whites from the North to arrest the attention of the press and the legislators. It would take whites from the North to catch the searching red eye of the TV cameras, to force their way into the Sunday sermon and the cocktail party chatter in Washington and New York. And it would take white hands reaching out that could help the Mississippi Negro struggle to his feet and stand erect. The risks of bringing white men and white women into this bastion of "white supremacy" were enormous. This calculated affront to the sensibilities and mores of the white society would evoke a response of applied pressure and harassment, and there was no way of avoiding it. The fear and hatred would not be mitigated because the northerners came nonviolently. To the Mississippi white the act of their coming was violence, and he prepared to resist this latest assault on his "Southern Way of Life." In Jackson the police chief built a military tank for fifty thousand dollars, calculated to defend law and order in the capital. Americans for the Preservation of the White Race, the town councils, and the Democratic Town Committees grouped their forces to resist the "mixers" who were coming to despoil and deflower. An inspired, reticent Negro who understood White America was going to force Mississippi to acknowledge her black children. No longer the truncheon in the isolated cell, the nameless black body being beaten and torn, the anonymous hooded terror. The whole world would be watching as Bob Moses led White America's children into Mississippi.

Moses let the wall take his weight. The muffled chatter of the hall murmured along the packed rows and ceased. The screen sprang to life and the last yellow bulb vanished.

In the darkness Mississippi ceased suddenly to be an abstraction. There, on the screen, brightly lit by an August sun, was Mississippi. A Negro girl, looking pert and resolute, walked down a dusty dirt road in a Negro quarter of a Mississippi town. The camera moved in and her intent face filled the screen.

"I want to vote so we can get some lights on our road, and get police protection."

A car passed behind her, a 1961 Ford, and the dust rose from the dirt road and caught the bright Mississippi sun. Now the camera moved and the documentary dissolved to the massive bulk of a white registrar of voters. The gross indolence of the body was accentuated by the cranky baby face which lolled on the fat, fleshy neck. The effect was startling and ludicrous. Here was a parody of "massive resistance." This overblown baby of a man had denied the vote to the Negroes of Tallahatchie County for years, and he was somehow at once hateful and ridiculous. A snicker of

The songs learned at Oxford sustained us all summer.

laughter raced through the hall, and a quick *"Shush!"* followed as the audience bent to hear. The cameras now moved through the "Sanctified Quarter" of Ruleville, Mississippi. An elderly Negro man, his leather face etched and tooled by seventy years of work in the fields, was quietly describing the horror of shotgun blasts that had torn into his living room. He showed the couch where two young girls had been cut down as they watched television. The hall was hushed, and a clearing of throats was the only sound that competed with the whirring of the overheated projector.

"I had driven to Indianola and applied to register to vote." The old man's gaze into the camera was steady. "I aim to go back to Indianola and apply again. Shooting's not going to turn me around."

The camera moved to the old Negro lady who was his wife. Her face was birdlike, and an absurd hat balanced on the top of her thin gray hair. The voice and the face conspired to conjure the image of an intent, bespectacled parrot, and her recital of the nightmare that had struck their home was lost as a nervous giggle ran through the seats. Again an angry *"Shush!"* and the eyes stayed riveted on the real citizens of Mississippi.

The lights came suddenly on as the film ended. The blinking students began to stretch and move in their seats. An enraged Negro strode down the aisle and leaped to the apron of the stage. His face was furious, and he quivered as he began to speak.

"You should be ashamed!" he growled. The students looked rapidly at their neighbors and back to the small intent figure that commanded the stage. "You could laugh at that film! Six of the Snick field workers left this hall when you laughed. They couldn't believe their ears, and neither could I."

His voice broke and tears glistened behind the glasses. With an effort of will he regained his control, and the words tore painfully from his throat.

"I hope by the end of this summer you will never laugh at such a film again."

The students looked stunned. What had happened? The dark figure on the stage was an accusing finger. Of what were they being accused?

Preiss and I moved out of the emptying hall and drove in silence to the beer cellar in town. He seemed excited by the evening, and when he finally settled into the corner of the booth, his voice was jubilant.

"It's classic! Here are these two very different groups. They're only alike in that they both think they understand the other, and certainly themselves."

He signaled for a pitcher of beer and placed his feet on the worn bench. His jaw moved with nervous excitement.

"They're both wrong."

The bartender came around the end of the bar carrying a foaming pitcher and two wet glasses to the booth. Preiss watched him silently and spoke again when the bartender had returned to his station.

"The students think they really understand these Snick kids. After all, here they are, making their commitment, ready to face the rednecks. Why? Because, they'll tell you, a great injustice has been perpetrated on the American Negro. They're coming to Oxford with their gift of a summer in their hands, and they want it to be an appreciated gift. They think they understand the Snick kids because they feel for the Mississippi Negro. A lot of them take the Friday night and Sunday morning morality seriously. So they really do feel for the Mississippi Negro."

He paused and studied the wet ring of suds on the table, carefully placing his glass exactly in the center. His eyes lifted to mine and he frowned.

"But they can't feel *like* the Mississippi Negro. They know it, and it makes them unhappy. Tonight they watched a fat man who was against letting Negroes vote in his district. They laughed at him because he looked grotesque and stupid. And when they saw a funny-looking little old lady who looked like a chicken, they laughed again. But when the lights came up and they heard that the Snick boys had walked out, they suddenly realized how insensitive their reactions had been. They don't like to find out they're insensitive about anything. Certainly not about Negroes! They were sure about that much—until tonight."

He lifted the glass and swallowed deeply. The beer left a faint trace of white on the sandy hairs of his moustache. He wiped it with the back of his hand and lit a fresh cigarette. "The Snick kids watched the same movie," he said. "But they saw different things."

"How could they see different things?" I asked. "Okay, these students are *not* Mississippi Negroes. Granted. But how different is their frame of reference about oppression and discrimination? After all, if they weren't sensitive to inhumanity, what brought them here?"

Preiss shook his head irritably. He moved the beer pitcher to my side of the table and filled my glass.

"How different? Listen. The Snick kids didn't see a fat man who was against Negroes. They saw a white man who was powerful, and he had hurt them. They knew this powerful white man. They knew he had hurt them, and they knew he would go on hurting them. This was no abstract injustice. This was the guy who said 'No' after you had worked your tail off for months getting frightened people to the point of walking up his county courthouse steps. This was "Mr. Charlie." This was no laughable fat man. This was the man you *weep* about. The Snick kids watched the volunteers laugh and they couldn't believe it. 'They're laughing! What are they doing here?' And then they watched the lady from Ruleville whose house and nieces got shot up. She's not funny-looking to them. They helped her wipe the blood off the couch and get her nieces into the hospital—the white hospital—because they couldn't stop the bleeding. And they watched these kids—mostly white kids—giggling at a ridiculous hat and a cackling voice. 'How can they laugh? What are they doing here?'"

Preiss, his face pale, wet his lips and ground out the cigarette. "These Snick workers have taken it for so long they didn't think they were sensitive anymore. They thought after the beatings and the grinding frustration they wouldn't feel pain anymore. They were sure about it—until tonight. The students laughed, and they found their nerves were exposed." He stretched his arms wide and arched his back. "Like I said." He grinned. "It's classic. And like I said this afternoon, they haven't really been listening."

He slid along the bench and stood up. "But tonight tore it. At last we can really start talking tomorrow."

We drove back to the campus and parked by the Administration building. We entered the foyer and immediately sensed that something was different. The center hall was deserted except for two students who stood at the entrance to the lounge. They leaned intently against the door-jambs, listening, and seemed completely unaware of our approach. Preiss glanced quickly at me and we moved swiftly across the hall and into the crowd that filled the room. It seemed that everyone was there. They sat hunched on the floor, knees drawn up, silent. The carpet was filled with students, and each leather lounge sofa and chair was hidden by the crush of bodies. All attention was directed at the two SNCC field workers who stood in the center of the crowd. The shorter, a wiry, very dark youngster in his early twenties, was weeping openly, and his words twisted out raw and savage.

"We love you—and we don't understand you! Sure we want you to come with us, but we're scared for you. You don't know the score—and we're scared for you. You can't know. You just can't know."

The words were alive and they moved into the room like a torn high-tension wire, sparking, leaping, and lethal.

"I was in the Army. They taught me how to hate and they taught me how to kill. But that's not what I need."

His voice broke, and he blinked as the tears moved down the dark, young cheeks. His hands were clenched tight against his thighs.

"I need to love you. We're going to Mississippi together, and I need to love you."

Time seemed to stop in the hushed hall. No one seemed to notice that the clock had pushed past midnight, for a torrent of love, heat, self-confessions, hopes, and fears swept the room in a violent flood of emotion. When he finished speaking—the pulsing rush of tumbling words suddenly ceasing—the second youngster began. His eyes were dry and his young brows knit intently as he sought voice for his fear. He started to speak, the words beating like nervous fingers on a bongo. He spoke in a cadenced rhythm, his voice expelling a sharp "hey" at the breathless end of each sentence. His eyes were troubled, and they seemed to beg understanding like a child, even as the staccato and stylized bop language made him sound worldly and citified. The students watched and listened, not quite knowing why they were not embarrassed by this public display of such profoundly private feelings. Instead they felt a great surge of relief, and their gratitude flowed like a released spring. This stripping of cool pretense, this humble reaching out of hands for common touch was a frightening and beautiful thing, and they felt for the first time a real sense of communication with these SNCC workers who were taking them away from home.

I looked at the two SNCC boys (I had thought they were young, but now for the first time I saw how vulnerable they were as well). They seem a breed apart, isolated guerrillas fighting a lonely battle for recognition and dignity. ("*Look* at me! I'm a man, too. *Look* at me!") They had been altered by their direct participation in the struggle, and this was what divided them from the kids listening. The volunteers were not removed from them by years, or even by race, for some of the students were Negro. They were removed by a searing experience that had stretched through

three years (not two months with an exit waiting). Tonight their deep
concern for these eager neophytes had swept away their defenses. The students' sense of exclusion and inadequacy was consumed in the heat of the
confessional. The terrible intensity of the stated commitments began to
forge a common bridge, for each in that room found an echo of his own
private fears. They started to *see* each other for the first time, and they
started, finally, to understand.

Bob Moses stood small and silent, his arm gently cradling the shoulder of his wife. She leaned like a heartbroken child against his side. Across
the room I saw Jim Forman standing silent on the edge of the crowd. He
looked spent and very young. This was the wonder, I thought, of SNCC.
Two half-educated, southern Negro kids had moved with a sure hand into
a crisis that might have torn apart the whole fabric of the summer. Their
instinctive sense of the right word and the right moment had illuminated
the room. The simple honesty of their grief and fear had acted as a catalyst
and transformed two suspicious groups into one. This was no prearranged
tactic of the leadership. It was the kind of gut response that had kept them
alive and resilient for three years. The room was on its feet now, arms
around the shoulders of the nearest neighbor, and the voices were one
voice. It rose and filled the lounge, a fervent and plaintive song that must
have echoed across the darkened campus.

I watched these kids as they swayed and sang. Faces were streaked
with tears and sweat, but their eyes were alive.

> *We've been 'buked*
> *And we've been scorned—*
> *We've been talked about*
> *Sure as you're bo-orn,*
> *But we'll never—*
> *No, we'll never turn back.*

John Strickland came back to the room as I lay feeling wound up and prickly. His black hair was plastered with sweat to his pale forehead. His eyes moved restlessly, and he looked stunned.

"Are you all right, John?"

He dropped onto the side of his bed and stared at me. A quiet, wondering smile moved across his white face and he nodded. "It's the first time I've ever been confronted by the raw force of love. It's quite a force.

3

The dining room wore an unmistakable "morning after" look. The morning light illumined the room, and talk bubbled at each large round table.

"I'll never forget last night," said the girl.

She bent to her coffee cup, and I noticed a long dark braid of hair which made her seem even younger than the rest at the table. She caught my eye and smiled shyly.

"It was like a gift."

The kids at the table paused over their food, and the large boy with the straw hair put down his glass of milk. He looked around the table.

"I'm glad we're all going together. I decided last night." He fished an envelope from his back pocket and he waved it at them. "My old man wrote me that the Mississippi papers are calling this an 'invasion.'" His eyes moved along the queue of students who were stacking their dirty dishes in the wire trays. "Some invaders!" he laughed.

A bored Negro busboy leaned against the counter, his eyes moving from the stacks of dirty cups to the clock at the end of the hall. I watched him lift a loaded tray and push backward into the kitchen. A wisp of steam escaped as the door swung closed behind him. The line moved forward, and the wire stacks were carefully refilled as the students moved, chattering, down the counter. The busboy reappeared from the damp steam of the kitchen. His sleepy eyes glanced from the clock to the loaded trays. He lifted the pile, moved backward against the swinging door, and paused. His eyes slid unseeing past the line of students and rested one more time on the clock. A line of Martin Luther King's made me smile: "Don't sleep through a revolution."

The brown face moved backward into the steam and the door swung shut.

"This is my second invasion," I said to the blond boy.

The talk at the table paused, and the young heads bent forward to listen.

"No kidding! Were you in Mississippi?"

"No," I said. "Normandy." I grinned at him. "World War Two."

The dark-eyed girl opposite carefully took a cigarette from the pack in her purse and lit it. Her eyes moved to mine and she said lightly, "You're very old." She smiled, but her eyes were bright and serious. "Were you frightened?"

"Of course. If you weren't scared, you didn't understand the situation!"

They laughed, but the girl pressed forward. "Could you work—being scared?"

"Honey," I said, "we won the war, and everybody was scared."

One of the boys leaned toward me. His sunburned face was frowning, and he rubbed his finger along a fresh shaving nick on his jaw. "Look. You say you were frightened. You were all frightened." He swallowed and looked hard at me. "Are you frightened now?"

The girl slowly ground out the cigarette in her saucer. The table was silent.

"As we used to say in the Navy, I'm 'scaired shit.' I'm older than you, and I understand the situation."

The boy nodded and rested back in his chair.

The tables were emptying, but the kids at the table hunched over their coffee. No one spoke, and they waited for me to continue.

"Listen. In the war I was a small-boat officer. Amphibious. I was in charge of six invasion craft. They were Higgins boats, half-inch plywood, and they were slow as hell. We mounted two thirty-caliber machine guns for the invasion, but the boats bounced so much you couldn't aim them. So we were sitting ducks and we all knew it. The night we left Salcombe for D-Day on our LST, I was so scared I couldn't sleep. There was a doctor on the ship, and we walked the wet decks for hours together. He had been through the invasions of North Africa, Sicily, and Salerno, and I asked him, like you're asking me, 'How can I keep from being so scared I won't do my job?' He laughed and said, 'It's simple arithmetic. Most guys don't get killed. Most guys don't get hit. If you're hit, most likely you're not going to get hit bad. If you're hit bad, most guys recover. So the odds are pretty good.' And I remember him looking at me on that blacked-out deck in the middle of the rough channel and asking me, 'Would you really want to be somewhere else tonight?' And I knew, really, that I didn't."

I looked at the faces of these boys and girls who were about to leave for Mississippi. (Was I really that young in Normandy?)

"You're here because you want to be." I smiled at their young, solemn faces. "But the arithmetic can help!"

The audience seemed restless. I was perched on the first step leading to the stage, watching the students and the energetic figure that moved back and forth behind the lectern. I put down my sketchbook and gave full attention to the students. They were intent, leaning on elbows against the chairs of the row ahead. Their fidgeting was not from boredom. The lecture the previous morning by the Negro educator had annoyed them because of the lack of scholarship. They knew more Negro history than he did, and they had been bored. But this morning they were irritated, and it showed itself in the sharp negative shakes of the head, in the angry rebuttal whispered to a neighbor. Reverend Lawson seemed to sense the antagonism. He paused for a brief moment, touched his lips with a white handkerchief, and then, frowning slightly, thrust ahead. He was an attractive young man, his rangy body controlled and athletic, and one felt a vitality that moved through him and lifted his words. He looked alert and at ease, but his voice snapped with conviction. He leaned toward the lectern on the balls of his feet, and one brown hand stabbed up and out as he challenged his audience.

"I tell you—there is a *power*, a real *power* in being good."

I had walked over from breakfast with the volunteers from my table. I knew they were thinking about surviving a summer in Mississippi. They had welcomed Lawson's lecture on nonviolence, for it was a tactic that might help them make it. Their displeasure now was the impatience of the pragmatist who is confronted with an idealistic theorizer. Unlike the volunteers, Lawson was a student of the whole philosophy of nonviolence. For him it was the light and the way, and he refused to deal with it as a tactical ploy. Power was important to the speaker and his audience, but I knew they read "power" very differently. I had listened to the talk in the lounges and at the dining tables, and I had come to realize that terms like "white power structure" had become alive and real to the volunteers. To them it conjured a vision of a tyranny that had imprisoned Mississippi and threatened their safety. This was "power" to them, and they wanted only to talk about ways of circumventing, upsetting, and disarming it.

Lawson pounded his fist into the other hand, and his voice rose. "Without a real moral growth you topple a political hack and replace him with another political hack. It's only by a real moral confrontation with

"There is a power, a real power in being good.

evil that you replace a bad society with a good one."

The questions erupted from the audience, and the anger was directed not at the minister but at a thesis that seemed mystical and theological at best, and hopelessly abstract at worst.

"We've got to get people the vote. Then they can 'morally confront' the power structure," argued a strident voice from the rear of the hall.

"Get people the vote!" snorted Lawson, "so they can send a Dawson from Chicago or a Powell from New York to Congress?"

The challenges and responses continued, and I glanced at the wall clock. The morning was being trapped in a swamp of personal theorizing. What would have been grist for a philosophy seminar was serving no affirmative function here, and it distressed me to see the gulf widening between this good man and the young people who wanted only to be told how best to perform good acts. Lawson stepped back from the apron of the stage and smiled ruefully at Bob Zellner who sat listening. He knew he had lost his audience, and he sensed that pursuit of semantic victory was pointless. He was a veteran of the first "sit-ins," and had been a passenger on the first "Freedom Rides." This was no fuzzy theologian selling "pie in the sky" to a rube congregation. He had witnessed the effectiveness of moral confrontation and had borne Christian witness to the disarming impact of love. But he sensed that a current was running here whose depth he could not plumb. He shrugged his shoulders and spread his hands parallel to the floor. As he nodded to Zellner to take the rostrum, a troubled smile seemed to flatten his mobile face. He stepped quickly to his seat and sat down.

Zellner sat for a moment, his elbows resting on his knees. He looked toward the rear rows and slowly moved his gaze down the hall. He found the last questioner and stood up. The morning sun played across the dusty stage from the tall east window and touched his straight blond hair. He looked like a college student home on holiday. Like the rest of the SNCC staff, he wore jeans and a blue work shirt. His usually smiling face was serious, and his soft, southern voice spoke gravely.

"Politics without morality is chaos," he said to the student.

He turned slightly toward Reverend Lawson who watched with narrowed eyes. A deep dimple moved fleetingly in Zellner's cheek, but he didn't quite smile.

"And morality without politics is irrelevant."

He thrust his hands into the rear pockets of his jeans, and he spoke with deliberate emphasis to the hushed hall.

"You must understand that nonviolence is essential to our program this summer."

His eyes were hard now, and the soft drawl had a cutting edge. "The program is more important than your hesitations. It is academic whether you embrace nonviolence philosophically or not. But if you are going to work in Mississippi with us this summer, you must be prepared to accept the ground rules. Whatever your reservations or hesitations may be in this, you can only act nonviolently in COFO."

His hands moved to his side and he stood motionless looking at the students. They listened, for this was one of them. They knew he had moved from a white campus in the South into the Movement, and they knew he had been arrested often and beaten by the police.

The strong, warm voice moved across the hall, gently splintering the hushed silence. "If you can't accept this, don't, please don't come with us."

Everyone stood in the June sunshine in front of the Administration building. The talk was muted, for we were all uneasy at what was about to take place. Kids smoked and shifted nervously as they watched the newsreel and television technicians lead wires and cables through the crowd and across the soft turf. I found Jack Preiss standing quietly on the edge of the lawn, arms folded, squinting in the bright glare of the sun.

"How do they do it, Jack?"

He nodded toward a group of staff who were working their way to the center of the crowd, carrying chairs from the dining hall over their heads.

"They'll set up a make-believe lunch counter. Then they'll integrate it!"

He laughed quietly. We watched as the crowd moved back, leaving a small cleared arena of grass.

A slight Negro youngster in a red turtle-neck sweater stepped into the center of the clearing. He held up his arms and the murmur of the crowd ceased. One suddenly heard the whir of the cameras.

"This is the way you protect your body," he said. His voice was flat. "The vital parts of your body are your head, your neck, and your groin. You can protect them best by curling up like a baby, your legs together, your knees pulled up to protect your gut and your privates, your hands and arms shielding your head and the back of your neck." He bent forward, rolling into a fetal position, his arms lacing across his bent head and his hands cradling the back of his head and neck. The girl next to me sucked in a deep breath. The boy rose from the lawn and led a volunteer from the press of bodies at the edge of the crowd.

"Let me see you protect yourself," he said.

The volunteer assumed the position and the staff man pulled back his sneakered foot, gently tapping the exposed areas of the supine volunteer.

"Your legs, your thighs, your buttocks, your kidneys, your back can take a kick or a billy club. So can your arms and your hands. Your head can't. Your neck can't. Your groin can't." The flat voice continued its dispassionate litany. "When your companion is being beaten or stomped while lying on the ground, you must protect him, or her. You do it by shielding his head with your body. Your back can take it."

Once more the demonstration, and again I became aware of the whine of the cameras. Everything would be recorded for the great spectator public except the nausea and the outrage of having to learn the arts of protecting yourself from American police who were waiting to assault you. I lifted my eyes from the red sweater of the staff worker. John Strickland stood ashen, staring at the lad curled up on the ground. Like the rest of the crowd, he was silent. Their eyes stayed riveted to the frozen tableau of a violence that till that moment had existed for them only in grade-B movies and tabloid spreads.

The afternoon was a nightmarish theatre, and the loveliness of that June afternoon would not be remembered by the students in the time ahead. The sky was a high delicate blue, and a sun-washed breeze played across the intent children play-acting on the green lawn.

The SNCC staff moved into their mock roles of white registrars, judges, paternalistic sheriffs, and frightened field hands with a sureness that was startling. They enacted the rituals of denial and humiliation they had learned from childhood, and no one had to coach a response or prompt a line. It was an incredible theatrical experience for me. But this was raw and unadorned, not a sublimation or transformation of life. This was the reality of the black man in white Mississippi. It was an afternoon that assaulted your sensibilities and moved you to anger and shame. The dry, bitter humor, the sardonic shrug, the earthy contempt, the endless guile of half-truth, the limitless capacity to ingratiate; all these were revealed naked and unashamed during those remarkable pieces of theatre. At one point a young Negro woman came to the "registrar" with her reluctant mother to try to register. The quick dismissal was side-stepped, and she persisted in pressing for the registration form. He exploded with anger.

"You get your goddam nigger ass out of my office!"

Once more the agile maneuvering by the girl, as she slid into a whining, feminine, ingratiating voice.

"Mistah Jameson, Suh, don' you remembuh me? Emmaline Jones? And my mama here, Aunty Lou? Why y'all talk to me like that, Mistuh Jameson, Suh? You knows us your whole life. Please, Suh, just the regis' papuh and and we'll be goin' home, Mistuh Jameson. How is Mastuh William and Miss Ann? My, what a pretty thing she is! Lawdy, I remembuh her Chrisnin'." The acrid, despised, and despising words hung in the air. Words set to curry the scorning condescension and approval of a master. We watched the sly transformation that turned his bright, Negro coed into a shuffling supplicant, a contemptible slattern using an ageless guile to ward off the blow of a white man.

The sun was dipping below tall elms that ringed the college, and the shadow of the Administration building wrapped the tiny stage and the intent audience. I remember the last sketch that was acted out on that June afternoon.

Two white volunteers and a SNCC worker approached the aged Negro who sat rocking on the make-believe porch. He watched the youngsters approach, sucked on his corncob pipe, and remained silent. The SNCC boy was first up the steps, and he paused respectfully before the old man.

"G'morning, Mr. Davis. How are you today?"

The old man continued to rock, but he removed the pipe and nodded his head. "Pretty well, Crosby. How's your daddy?"

"Feelin' much better now, Mr. Davis. I expect you'll see him at the chapel on Sunday. Mr. Davis, I'd like you to meet two friends of mine, John Suter and Jim Dann. John and Jim have come down here to work on the voter registration with us, Mr. Davis. Jim here goes to college way out west in Oregon, and John is studying at Wesleyan, up North—in Connecticut."

Jim stepped forward and extended his hand.

"I'm very happy to meet you, Mr. Davis."

The old man started to rise from the chair and very tentatively took the white hand in his own. I watched Jim Forman playing the role of this bent, reticent, field hand. The strangeness felt by a Mississippi Negro who is approached by a white man who treats him with deference was transmitted to the whole crowd.

The white volunteer shook his hand and said, "Mr. Davis, we hope you and your two sons will go with us to the courthouse in Clarksdale on Saturday. We're all going to drive down together in the morning. I know you understand how important it is for you all to register to vote this summer."

Forman resumed his rocking and carefully relit his pipe. He was polite and attentive, but he made it clear that he was not about to let his boys go down to the courthouse on Saturday or any day.

"Well, we'll have to see, Mr. Dann. Votin's never been our concern. We has all we can do to chop enough to get through the winter. My boys are good boys. But they got a lot to do right here on the place."

All the canny delays and evasions, the whole bureau full of the ancient nostrums guaranteed to make you survive in a white man's land were skillfully displayed by Forman. Never once the exaggeration that would tear the mood or turn the moment into a dialect parody. As I watched this sophisticated man move so effortlessly into a primitive role, I began to see and understand. The Negro in American society has been acting since he was weaned. The subtle nuances of a theatrical craft and discipline are blood and bone of a race response, a ghetto memory. They are the daily lessons of the alleys, the employment offices, the backs of buses, the "nigger-heavens," the "nigger churches." They conspire to protect the Negro from being hurt, from being destroyed, and in the process we have come to know only the façade that says "Negro." Like a lovely moth shedding its cocoon, layer upon layer, the beautiful complexity of the person beneath the façade began to emerge for me that afternoon. As if for the first time, I began to see the people. Not victims, I thought. Not causes. Not heroes. Not colored people. Not Negro people.

I raised my head and looked across the crowd. Charles McLaurin leaned against a pillar at the entrance to the building. He looked ill, and I knew that his teeth were still loose from the beating two weeks before. His dark glasses shielded his eyes, but I could see him wince as he touched his jaw tenderly.

Not heroes, I thought. Not Negro heroes. People.

Part II
GREAT GOD, I'M ON MY WAY

4

I stared from the airplane window till the horizon suddenly tilted and was lost behind the lifting tip of the wing. I closed my eyes, thinking of the two days I had had with June and the kids in Connecticut. Good. Real good. The week end had been full of the sentiment that goes with a high school graduation. Dick and Laurie had been great, keeping it light, masking their concern for the weeks ahead with affectionate teasing. As Dick had adjusted his graduation robe, his eyes met mine. "How do you like my generation, old man?"

For two days June and I had talked, eager to share all I had seen and felt at Oxford. My going to Mississippi was not my commitment. It was ours. Knowing it, I held back nothing. The doubts and fears I had, the opportunity I perceived to make a small contribution through my reportorial drawings, the jolting impact of the committed kids at Oxford. All of it. For I knew I could not spare her by kidding her. Her strength lay in an uncompromising honesty which allowed her to see things as they are. Her clarity of vision did not permit distortions, and I knew that for her there would be no blinking at the dangers of the summer. She had curled up in the crook of my arm that lazy Sunday morning before I left for the airport. Her voice was soft, and it broke just once. "Don't worry about us. We'll be here. Hold on tight."

I stepped from the plane and stood for a moment at the top of the steps. The Memphis depot was modern, elegant, and quite deserted. I searched quickly among the few faces awaiting the plane's arrival and was disappointed that Dale Gronemeier was not there. The air-conditioned plane had not prepared me for the damp blanket of heat that met me as I descended the ramp and crossed the glaring concrete to the terminal. By the time I had reclaimed my luggage, I was feeling edgy. The airplane coffee tasted metallic and sour in my mouth, and my legs and back felt wet under the weight of my cotton suit. The black and yellow Hertz sign was at the rear of the terminal, and I started toward it across the marble floor.

"Tracy!" A sweat-shirted figure was trotting toward me.

I put down the bag and grabbed the outstretched hand. "Man, am I glad to see you, Dale!"

He grinned back. His nose was red and peeling, and his khaki pants were sooty and oily from the motorcycle.

"I had a wild ride down from Ohio. But beautiful! How was the graduation?"

"A critical success. He made it. All's well in Connecticut. Come on. Let's get us a car and go to Mississippi."

The lady at Hertz was blond and pretty. Yes, we have a car for you. No, we don't have any with Mississippi plates. I'm absolutely certain. The voice had altered subtly. "Why don't you try one of the other agencies?"

Her eyes flicked at Dale and returned to me. "You planning a long trip?"

"Several weeks," I said. "Thank you. I'll check the other agencies."

She folded her arms and watched us move to the other rental offices. No, sir. No car with Mississippi plates. No, sir. No car at all. The cool blonde still stood, arms crossed, as we returned to the Hertz counter.

"Ma'am," I said. "I'd like to rent a car with Tennessee plates."

Deadpan, she reached for the form and filled it out. Without a word she pushed it toward me and held out a pen for me to sign. As I thanked

Loyola teacher Dale Gronemeier, Communications Director for the
Ruleville project.

her, a small smile flitted across her face. "Y'all will find the car parked
across the road in front of the building."

She paused just a moment, leaned back against the file, and crossed
her arms again. "It's a yella Chevvy. With Tennessee plates."

I picked up the receipt form and placed it carefully in my wallet. As
I turned to pick up my bag, she spoke again. "Y'can't fool 'em, y'know."

"No, ma'am. I guess not. A yella Chevvy, you said." I grinned at her
and lifted my bag. Dale was already halfway to the door.

Dale pulled alongside, his Honda dusty and panting quietly. "I'm
leaving the bike in Reverend Lawson's garage in Memphis. Follow me."
We wound our way along the wide boulevards and stopped finally in
front of a large, plain brick church. Dale swung from his bike and mounted
the porch of the frame house next door. A young white man followed him
down the steps, unlocked the chain wire gate that sealed the driveway, and
swung it open. He waved us in. Dale gunned his cycle and spun up the
drive and into the open garage. The young man introduced himself to me.
He was muscular and rangy, and his manner was boyish.

"I'm assisting Reverend Lawson this summer." He said it with a good
deal of pride. "He's a fine minister, and a great man in the Movement. It's
a wonderful experience working here with him. Are you both on the way
in to Mississippi?" We nodded.

"Have you been there before?" he asked.

"No," I said. "Have you?"

"Yes. A number of times earlier this year. But lately I've been involved
right here in Memphis. Memphis has a ways to go, but it's a pretty civi-
lized town and it's getting there. I'll tell you something. After you've been
a while in Mississippi, you'll feel like you're back home when you get north
to Memphis!"

He smiled as we climbed back into the car. "As they'd say down here,
'That's a right pretty yellow!'"

We shook hands, and he leaned for a second against the fender. "If it
gets too pressured, come see us for a week end."

We backed from the driveway and he carefully relocked the fence. I
watched him in my rearview mirror. He put his arm around a Negro child,
and they started up the steps to the parsonage as I turned the corner.

The neat geometry of the Delta unfolded as we moved at a cautious
fifty-five into the heartland of Mississippi. Dwarfed cotton plants
stretched in symmetric rows almost to the horizon, the dark soil between

the rows cartwheeling, black spokes as the Chevvy moved swiftly down the bright ribbon of road.

Dale stretched his legs under the dashboard and looped an arm carelessly over the back of the seat. The attitude of repose was deceptive, for his eyes were quick and alert, scanning the road carefully ahead and searching the road behind for any approaching vehicle.

"Hey, man, slow down. I want to read the sign coming up." He chuckled as I lifted my foot from the accelerator. "Welcome to the Magnolia State!"

I studied the rearview mirror and saw only the sun-baked two-lane highway stretching north toward Memphis. The sun was at its height, and the road shimmered and wavered in the heat. I pumped the gas pedal, and the Chevvy raced down the deserted pavement.

"Take it easy," Dale cautioned. "There's a car coming toward us, and the Highway Patrol must be moving up and down this route."

My eye moved once more to the mirror, once more to the road ahead, once more to the shivering needle of the speedometer. Once more I eased to fifty-five, and for the first time I was beginning to feel the tension in my neck. The car approaching moved out of the overheated light and turned out to be a green Ford pick-up truck. Two white men wearing wide, straw farmer's hats studied our license and squinted at us as the truck whooshed past. As I read my mirror, the man next to the driver turned and watched us move away.

Dale sensed my concern, and he leaned silently across the seat for some moments, watching the Ford grow small in the distance.

"They're gone," he said finally. "But watch your speed."

"I'm watching my speed. Christ, I've never watched my speed so carefully in my life. I'm getting a stiff neck watching my speed."

The windows were rolled down, and the heavy scented air pushed softly through the car.

"What difference does it really make if I'm going fifty-five or sixty-five?" I asked. "If the Mississippi Highway Patrol decides to arrest me and they say I'm going seventy-five, then I'm going seventy-five." I glanced across at Dale. "So why am I breaking my neck going fifty-five?"

Dale laughed. "You're the kind of guy Jess Brown was talking about last Thursday in Oxford."

I remembered, and I laughed with him. Jess Brown, a stringy, grizzled Negro lawyer from Jackson, Mississippi, had been describing the state's judicial process and what we might expect from the State Police. Brown was one of only three lawyers in Mississippi who would accept a civil rights case. All three were Negroes. His bright eyes snapped with a malicious humor, and he regarded the world from under his craggy brows like a savage sparrow. His bony fingers seemed always in motion; brushing back his drooping moustache, waggling in the air to punctuate a point, rolling a cigar. His face was mobile and weathered, a hook nose jutting boldly out from the network of lines that creased his skin. Brown's neck was corded and skinny, and his collar and his suit seemed to be a size too large. When the questioning from his bright, college-boy audience began, he sat down, elaborately lit his cigar, and regarded the first questioner from behind a flame that he struck from a stove match.

Many of the students were knowledgeable about constitutional law, and this one was not embarrassed to let the rest of the hall know it. Brown blew a cloud of blue smoke and flicked the ash from the cigar. He rose, a tough, aging bantam, and walked carefully to the edge of the stage. He smiled gently at the student.

"Son, a Mississippi highway at midnight is no place to teach a Mississippi policeman with two years of education the fine points of constitutional law! You just go along with the man and don't say nothin'. And in the morning you try and get ahold of one of us."

Dale laughed in recollection and said, "You might just as well

"Son, a Mississippi highway at midnight is no place to teach a Mississippi policeman with two years of education the fine points of constitutional law!" –Jess Brown, Mississippi lawyer.

not give them excuses for stopping us they don't already have." He leaned forward and squinted at the sign which stood boldly alongside the highway. "IMPEACH CHIEF JUSTICE EARL WARREN!" Dale read aloud, "Signed, The John Birch Society."

"Welcome to the Magnolia State, Gronemeier!" I drawled.

By the time we reached Aaron Henry's drugstore in Clarksdale we were damp with sweat and parched. We stood blinking by the car and looked about us for Lafayette Sirney or Jim Jones who were the co-leaders of the Clarksdale district. A handful of Negroes stood on the corner and watched us with frank interest as we moved toward the Fourth Street Pharmacy. I looked hurriedly up and down the block, and pushed open the door.

Lafayette stood just inside. His usually cherubic face was serious and concerned as he dropped a dime into the phone. He looked toward the door as we entered, grinned, and held up a finger in greeting. Once more he cocked his head, frowned, and talked very carefully into the phone. "I'm calling to find out what the charges are against the three boys and a girl who were arrested today."

His attention shifted from the mouthpiece of the telephone to us. He squinted his eyes and shook his head. He smiled wryly and hung the receiver back on the hook.

Jim Jones waved from the door and joined us at the counter.

"I saw your car down the block. I'm glad you made it down okay. Oh, my! A yellow Chevvy!" He laughed. "I hope it moves!"

Lafayette came across the room and shook hands.

Jim asked quietly, "What did you find out?"

"They keep pickin' 'em up. Two this morning and two this afternoon. *Wham!* The minute they hit the street. All they'd tell me was they were bein' held. Oh yeah, and to stop botherin' 'em on the phone or they'd have my nigger ass!"

Jim frowned and he nodded at Dale and me. "Have a drink and we'll get going to Ruleville."

A youngster behind the counter poured Coca-Cola syrup from a gallon jug into the glasses, added water and ice, and carefully stirred. He handed us the drinks and stood listening to our conversation. I knew that Aaron Henry's Fourth Street Pharmacy was the center of civil rights activity in that area of Mississippi, and anyone working there must be part of the Movement. The store was a natural target for the racists' reprisals, and I knew that only recently the front plate glass had been blown out. I looked at the slender fourteen-year-old behind the counter and wondered how you learned his nonchalance. I glanced at the rear of the store for a glimpse of Aaron Henry, but the prescription counter was empty. I was disappointed that he was not there. I had read about this stubborn man who refused to be intimidated. His store windows continued to carry the Emancipation Proclamation, and I knew it was an ulcerating reminder to Police Chief Ben Collins that an indomitable spirit remained in Clarksdale.

Jim Jones looked thoughtfully into his glass, and his Indian face was serious as he turned to Lafayette.

"Call Jackson and let them know who's been picked up. Tell them we don't know the charges yet. They may want to send a lawyer right up. Collins is trying to frighten the workers, and he's probably succeeding. I don't think he'll hold them long. Meanwhile we better keep off the streets." He walked to the door and watched a police car edge slowly down the block. "I'm going to Ruleville and see Mac." The police car crept around the corner. "We better move out," he said.

I left change on the counter and waved to Lafayette who was once more stationed at the phone.

"I'll see you soon," he called. "Ruleville's my home town!"

Once more the car was moving south on Highway 41. Jones and

McLaurin had agreed in Oxford that Jim should drive with me to
Ruleville. A Negro was sitting with me and we were driving south through
the Mississippi Delta. The feeling of exposure I was to know so often in
those first days made me feel edgy. Did Jim feel as vulnerable as I, I wondered? Maybe it would be safer if he sat in the back seat so that approaching cars might not notice. I was ashamed at the thought and moved my
eyes to scan the road ahead. Why, dammit, should it even occur to me?
Joe Louis's classic line about Max Schmeling popped into my head, and I

Highway 41, Ruleville, Mississippi.

found myself grinning. "He can run," rumbled Joe, "but he can't hide!" If I was to function this summer and not be maimed by a timid caution, I must decide that just as I would not hide, neither would I run. A pickup truck with a long antenna waving from its rear bumper cut in from a crossroad and moved alongside. The white, impassive face looked long and hard. I kept the Chevvy at fifty-five and returned the searching look. A shotgun and rifle were riding easily in a cradle behind the driver's head. The truck finally moved past, picking up speed.

I heard Dale exhale a long breath. "Is the antenna for a two-way radio?" he asked.

Jones turned in his seat and nodded. He smiled across at me. "They know you're here. Let's see what this baby can do."

The road behind me was empty, and in the clear afternoon light I could see the pick-up truck turn off and race up a dirt road. The cloud of dust kicked up lay yellow in the air, and the truck disappeared finally behind the low outbuildings of a plantation.

We turned left off 41 soon after we entered Ruleville and eased onto a dirt road that led alongside an open field. Beyond the field a spanking new brick hospital, low and modern, faced the highway, and at the far end of the field a bright covey of monoplanes used for spraying were neatly lined up. Across from the field, two hundred yards off Highway 41, stood a white, white, frame building. Three worn wooden steps led to a double door. Over the entrance a gooseneck pipe held a single hundred-watt bulb. The windows were reflecting the late afternoon sun, the golden western light the only adornment on the stark modesty of the building. The small yard was a patchwork of dirt and clumps of grass. It looked weary.

Jim scanned the building and shook his head. "Mac must be at the Hamers'. Nobody here at Williams Chapel."

We drove into the Sanctified Quarter, named for the Sanctified Church. The houses were small, neat, most of them white with a colored trim, a few in obvious and desperate need of repair. Their porches sagged, and broken steps were propped by cement blocks. But, in the main, the neighborhood was cheerful and pleasant. Zinnias and geranium fronted most of the homes, and a garden patch usually stretched to meet the kitchen garden of the neighbor on the next block. One could see bean-poles, tomato stakes, small rows of corn, and fresh wash. An air of peace lay over this rural neighborhood. A cloud of dust stirred behind the car and followed, mottling the dry green hedges as it settled. I nodded and tooted at some of the kids that scattered from their play to watch, saucer-eyed, as we drove through the quarter. A few of the older children whooped and ran briefly alongside. The older folks in rockers and on front steps acknowledged my wave with a polite and noncommittal nod.

Jim pointed to a white, frame house that was partly hidden from the road by an immense pecan tree. "Pull off the road and park in the empty yard on the left. They're all there under the tree, and Mac's with them."

McLaurin gave a big grin as he watched me pull in. He walked up to the Chevvy and patted the rear fender lovingly. "We sure can use that!" he said.

"It's my most important contribution to the Civil Rights Movement, and Mr. Hertz's. Even if it is yellow!"

"It moves pretty good," said Jim.

We crossed the road and moved instinctively to the deep shade of the pecan tree. The air was heavy with heat and the whirring murmur of the insects seemed to throb as I squatted in the shadow.

"We're all here now," said Mac. "Eighteen—until the Freedom School and community center folks get here next week."

The kids stretched out under the tree looked unkempt and uncertain. The fatigue of the long trip from Oxford showed plainly in their young faces. They waved and called hellos to Dale and me, but the talk was desultory. The blouses of the two girls in the group were stained with sweat, and the boys, mopping their flushed faces, stripped to their T shirts. Mac, alone, moved comfortably about the group, squatting here and there to answer questions. A faint film of perspiration shone on his dark skin, but his movements were easy, and one knew that the heat of the day never entered his mind. The physical discomfort and spiritual disquiet I had sensed in him at Oxford seemed now to have been discarded. His walk was light, and for the first time McLaurin seemed to me to be a man at peace with himself. He threw back his head and laughed at something that Jones had said, and I wondered at the layers of complexity in this youngster. He made his way to the steps of the porch where Dale and I sat.

"I'm not sure where you're going to stay eventually, Dale," he said. "Maybe here at the Hamers'. But for now you and Tracy will stay over in Jerusalem Quarter, across the highway, with the Williams. Once communications are set up you'll need a phone, and this will probably be headquarters at the beginning."

Jim Jones came over and extended his hand. "I'm heading back to Clarksdale. Got a ride headin' north."

"Good luck," I said, thinking of the four arrests already made by Ben Collins. "Will I be seeing you again soon?"

He shrugged and grinned. "It's likely. So long, Mac."

McLaurin rubbed his chin and nodded slightly. "Take it easy, man." Jones turned and trotted toward the highway.

McLaurin opened the Chevvy door and called to the group who listened attentively from under the tree.

"We'll all meet at William Chapel at seven-thirty. Mass meetin' tonight!"

The volunteers scrambled to their feet. In twos and threes they moved down the dusty road, some breaking off to climb a porch step and disappear into their new homes. The eyes of the Negros followed them as they moved, and the children giggled as some of the students called "Hi!"

The two girl students moved easily down the road. A couple of Negro children, holding hands, zig-zagged after them, laughing when one of the girls would turn and catch their eye. Three Negro women stood at a porch step, their faces shadowed by the wide straw hats they wore. One had been watering a despondent, straggling petunia in a coffee tin, and she paused as she noticed the girls approaching.

"Hi!" called Gretchen. "Is it always this hot in Ruleville?"

The deep shade of the pecan tree in the Hamer yard.

"How do," chorused the women softly. The one with the watering can stepped to the hedge and the girls stopped. "It is right hot this afternoon. I expects it will cool some when the sun goes down yonder in an hour," she said.

"That's good!" said Gretchen laughing. "I don't want to melt completely away my first day in Mississippi!"

Donna waved at the woman as they resumed their walk down the road to Mrs. Sisson's house. "See you at the meeting!"

The two women joined the third who held the watering can. They were looking down the road after the girls as I passed them.

We stepped gingerly on the two short plants that crossed the shallow drainage ditch and started across the small front yard. I looked at my new home. It was a small, low house, covered with an imitation, mustard-colored brick. I groaned when I noticed the roof. It was corrugated iron, and I knew it must be an oven inside. Perched on an ancient, listing table in the yard were a variety of houseplants, set out for the summer. A splash of zinnias made the yard cheerful, and they led along the side of the house to a garden in the rear. As I glanced up the block I noticed that the house next door was an immaculate, white clapboard. Its trim was freshly painted, and a television antenna stood astride the blue shingled roof. A bright-eyed ten-year-old leaning against a shiny Pontiac in the driveway was solemnly watching us. Peering from behind the car were a scattering of younger children. The boy held a softball, and an immense glove dangled from his other wrist.

When I called "Hi!" he turned, giggling to his friends.

"Roy! You get in here for supper. Now!"

He fled across the yard, the glove flapping from his wrist. At the top of the steps he paused, grinned, and disappeared inside.

5

I followed Dale as Mac held open the screen door. We stepped into the warm shadow of Mrs. Williams' living room. She stood at the door as we moved, blinking, inside, wiping her hands on the striped apron that was tied around her ample middle. Mahogany skin glowed in the dim light of the room, but a bright reflection from the doorway was caught on the panes of her glasses. The lens of one was cracked horizontally across the center, but the fractures could not disguise the wide-eyed, humorous appraisal she was giving me. Her head tilted back, for she was quite short, and she took my extended hand with a warm smile. "Why, I'm so glad to meet you! Won't y'all come in and set down for a while?" She pulled some rockers near the open door where there was a chance for a whisper of breeze.

"How have you been, Mac-Laurin? I ain't seen you since you got back from Ohio." She gave a sly, sideways smile at McLaurin, full of playfulness and affection. "Don' hardly seem the same with Mac-Laurin holdin' meetin's at the Chapel. Girls been askin' for you, Mac-Laurin. When's Mac-Laurin comin' back? When's Mac-Laurin comin' back?" She watched him flush with embarrassment and her head rocked back. She hooted with laughter.

"We're havin' a meetin' tonight," he mumbled and then grinned. "We'll sing up a storm, even without Mrs. Hamer!"

"This is my husban', James," said Mrs. Williams in a tender voice. "These are the gennemen who are going to stay with us, Jim."

He stood quietly in the doorway, a spare, bald, bright-eyed man of seventy-nine. His bony, old man's chest was visible beneath his white underwear shirt, but his arms and hands still showed the corded, cabled muscles of a young man. A small paunch on his wasting frame seemed out of place. His brown feet padded unshod across the aged linoleum in a slow, old man's walk, and he shook hands silently with Dale. When he reached me, he took my hand in his, and I felt the worn and calloused skin press mine with a surprising gentleness.

"I'm very pleased to meet you, Mr. Williams. It's very generous of you and Mrs. Williams to open your house to us this way."

His head shook slightly, and I saw tears start behind his wire-framed glasses. He opened his mouth in a vain effort to speak, looked deeply into my eyes, and shook his head. His eyes dropped, and his hand softly released mine. He made his way from the room in the same silence with which he had entered. McLaurin watched him leave and rose to go. Mrs. Williams swung open the screen door and said as he passed, "We're gonna have some supper and come along to the meetin'. You got supper somewhere, Mac-Laurin?"

"Yeah." He nodded and waved his hand briefly as he stepped into the golden light that flooded the road.

Mr. James Williams' home, Ruleville.

Mrs. Williams led Dale and me through the small house. I could hear a child cooing in the small room that led from the kitchen, and a whispering murmur of an old man's voice. Mrs. Williams turned to us and smiled. "Our granddaughter, Sharon, is jus' getting' up from her nap. Brother James is changin' her." She swept a dishtowel from a wire line that was suspended across the room, and in a single movement thrust it into a storage bin that stood against the wall. The room was scrubbed and spotless, and the faint smell of Flit gave an aseptic fragrance.

"This is my kitchen," she said, cocking her head and appraising it as if for the first time. There was no hint of apology or embarrassment in the statement. This battered kitchen was but one more item in Rennie Williams' long life that was full of used clothing, mended utensils, and staggering tables—a patchwork of the possible.

The small window that faced the garden was slid back, and the kitchen door was opened wide in a forlorn hope of capturing some vagrant breeze. The pitch of the iron roof was low, and the tiny room was stifling.

I glanced through the screen and saw Roy catching the softball as he rolled the ball endlessly up the blue shingled slope of roof. "Who lives next door, Mrs. Williams?"

She wheeled from the stove where she stood stirring a boiling pot. "Teacher," she snorted. "A scaird teacher!"

The old gas stove and an older refrigerator shone against the stained ochre of the composition walls. A heavy-legged wooden table, listing slightly, stood in the center of the tiny room. Leaning against the wall was a peeling cupboard on whose shelves were piled neatly an oddly mismatched assortment of cups, saucers, glasses, and plates. The shining, chipped crockery mimicked the light that shone wanly from the forty-watt bulb that hung suspended over the table. A water tap leaked drops

Ruleville interior: my bedroom.

Mr. James Williams.

Mrs. James Williams.

of water into a bucket on the floor in a sullen, halting pat, pat, pat. I realized with surprise that there was no sink.

Next to the stove was a crowded worktable, full to overflowing with condiments, cooking utensils, and a double boiler holding empty baby bottles and nipples. A bunch of carrots, the dirt still clinging damply to the orange skin, rested in a colander with a pile of yellow snap beans. Two ancient dishrags hunt drying on a hook over the stove. Mrs. Williams turned the flame lower under the pot, stooped with a grunt to pick up two plastic dishes left by Sharon, and led us into the tiny room in the rear. A high double bed seemed to overflow the room. Wedged in a corner was a bulging bureau. Two half-open drawers showed that it held the Williams' "go to meeting" clothes. A tired dressing table hugged the wall, reflecting the window that opened on the garden. I stooped beneath the low pitch of the roof and looked out through the patched screen. A weathered coop of ancient gray lumber harbored a strutting cock that puffed and gurgled. Two lines were heavy with bed linen and a covey of Sharon's tiny underpants. Beyond stretched a half-dozen rows of vegetables. The acrid smell of zinnias that nestled beneath the coop and the window was pleasant, and I hoped this snug room might be mine. I followed Dale back into the parlor and examined the room carefully as I leaned against the back of a rocker. The room was the coolest in the house, and the largest. Its walls were alive with photographs of smiling sepia teen-agers in cap and gown. Over a gas space heater was a large brown picture of Mr. and Mrs. Williams in an oval frame. A young, solemn man in his twenties stood gazing at the room, his tentative smile frozen forever on the yellowing paper. A slim, eager woman, her eyes bright and her round face self-conscious in an attitude of rigid attention stood beside him. I glanced at Mrs. Williams who was proudly introducing us to her two sons and a daughter from the smiling young faces of three Ruleville graduating classes. Her figure had sagged and overflowed since the bridal year of the picture, and the dark, neat bun of hair in the picture was now a rough mixture of salt and pepper that tended to come loose and stray. She brushed back a lock which fell damply across her forehead and sat down in a rocker which creaked heavily under her. She caught my look, and I realized with a shock that only her eyes were as before. They remained wide and clear, full of the devil and a challenging kind of pride. We pulled up chairs and sat down with her.

"Are you sure that we're not putting you and Mr. Williams out of your bed?" I asked.

"No suh!" she said vehemently. "Brother Williams and I really does prefer that room in there with Sharon. You two are so welcome to these two rooms."

"We hate inconveniencing you both," said Dale.

She gave a lingering look at Dale and said, "You ain't inconveniencing us none." Her eyes glistened. "We're just so glad you come, it's the least we can do. When Mac-Laurin asked us if we'd take you folks in last spring, I told him. 'We's poor folks, Mac-Laurin,' I said. 'We ain't got very much.

But what we got, we wants to share with these folks who're leavin' their comfortable homes and families to come help us.'" She rose with an effort from the chair. "We's mighty glad the good Lord sent you to us." She trudged across the worn linoleum and left us to prepare supper.

I stretched and tilted my feet against the end of the double bed. "Home is where the heart is, Gronemeier."

He looked thoughtfully at the door that led to the kitchen. His head nodded. "She's nice."

"Who's going to take which room, kid?" I asked. "This is cooler, but it's nearer the road. You want to be cooler or safer?"

Dale pulled off his wet sweatshirt and grunted. "I'd rather be cooler."

"Fine," I agreed happily, grabbing my suitcase and heading for my little room away from the road.

I swung my grip onto the bed and was unpacking my sketchbooks when I heard Mr. Williams approach the room.

"Come on in, Mr. Williams," I called. He paused at the door.

"I'm sorry I couldn't welcome you befo', Mr. Sug-man." His voice was an old man's voice, gentle and a little uncertain, and he made an effort to control it. His bright eyes blinked and he continued. "I was jus' so filled up, meetin' you and Mistuh Dale in my house, I couldn't talk."

His voice was stronger now, and he stood very straight. "It's a fine, Christian thing, a fine thing that you all have come here." He shook his head wonderingly, and his glance moved to my plaid suitcase. "McLaurin told us you have a family at home." His voice quavered, and he cleared his throat. "It's a fine thing, your coming," he said huskily. His bald head was nodding as he left the room.

Dale smiled across the table at Mrs. Williams. The kitchen was cooler now, and we had washed up and changed clothes. The sun was down and a sweet dusk moved into the room.

"Do you say 'Grace,' Mrs. Williams?"

A pleased look darted from Mrs. Williams to her husband, and they both nodded, smiling. She clasped her hands and rested her forehead against them. Mr. Williams closed his eyes, and his lips moved soundlessly as Mrs. Williams' deep voice filled the room.

"We thanks you, Lord, for the blessin's of food on our table, and for sendin' us these good people to share our burdens. We asks Thy grace on our house and on our friends here who are so far from their loved ones at home. We asks it in the name of Thy sweet son, Jesus. Amen."

6

I settled into a corner of the tiny platform that held the lectern, and sketched my first "mass meeting." Williams Chapel was alive now, and the wooden theatre seats were almost all filled. The students looked fresh and alert, their faces beginning to flush in the crowded room. They looked expectantly about them and smiled. The Negroes seated near them returned their smiles shyly and dropped their eyes. Mrs. Williams sat comfortably in the front row, a fan from the local funeral parlor moving steadily in her hand. Her face was damp with sweat, and the dark skin shone in the light of the two naked bulbs that lit the room. She sat in a group of elderly women who chattered and watched, their fans flipping continuously.

I looked about the hall. The walls were bare but for a number of pennants proclaiming "Banner Offering Class," and a poster-sized book of illustrated Bible stories which hung from a clothes hook in the rear of the hall. Behind the pulpit was a threadbare American flag draped across the window. A single poster showing children facing hoses in Birmingham proclaimed "We Shall Overcome."

McLaurin stood facing the room, his arms folded, listening to Mrs.

Irene Johnson, the community leader. She nodded to neighbors and pointed out new arrivals to McLaurin. Many of them looked quickly about them as they stepped inside, and moved inconspicuously to the side or rear. Two rows in the front on the left were filled with teen-age girls, their bright cottons in pastel pinks and yellows lighting up the front of the chapel. They put their heads together and smothered giggles, their eyes darting around the room, missing nothing. The boys drifted in and out of the doors, uncertain whether or not to stay. They would stand briefly in clusters at the back of the room, looking uncomfortable. A few middle-aged men were seated on the edge of the congregation near the windows, and a scattering of elderly men sat fanning themselves near the exit in the rear. But the large part of the hundred and twenty seats were taken by women. Mrs. Johnson smiled, and nodded and waved, and her suppressed excitement was communicated to them all. "This," she seemed to say, "is going to be special."

The texture of that first meeting in Ruleville *was* very special. In a summer of mass meetings the green seedling promise of that hot night in Williams Chapel remains fresh in memory. For Mrs. Williams, Mrs. Johnson, and old Joe McDonald this must have been a breathtaking event in the brown and even pattern of their days. Here was youth, smiling, kind, smart youth! And not just the scrubbed whites, whites like they had never known, but their own. Their glistening eyes would settle on John Harris and Charles McLaurin, and you knew that these were their very special knights. These were the new folk heroes of the Delta.

McLaurin called the volunteers to the front, and they ranged across the slightly raised stage facing the audience. Their presence brought a vicarious sense of certainty and well being to the impoverished little hall, and they seemed handsome and impregnable. McLaurin's dark glasses moved from the stage to the hushed seats.

"I'll let them introduce themselves to you."

"Mr. Charlie's not goin' to like it, but we're goin'!"

Charles McLaurin leads first meeting in Williams Chapel.

"I'm Dennis Flanagan, University of Washington."

"I'm Gretchen Schwarz, Swarthmore College."

"I'm George Winter, Ione, California."

"I'm Donna Howell, University of New Mexico."

"I'm John Harris, Howard University."

Their vitality seemed to fill the church. Together they reflected an unharried America. Their open faces seemed to speak a kind of radiant confidence that comes through the skin to the nation's favored children.

"I'm Larry Archibald, Harvard College."

"I'm Len Edwards, University of Chicago."

"I'm Charley Scattergood, Washington."

Their faces were flushed with heat, and their fresh shirts were beginning to spot with sweat. No one but they knew the fear and the wondering, the nagging questions with which they had lived the last weeks. As they met Ruleville, they searched the audience. For the first time the enormity of their commitment stood visible. They read it in every face that looked toward them. It was manifest in every youngster's unblinking gaze and in every moist eye of the adults. It was in the old, mended clothes, on the peeling boards, the rickety splintered chairs. *Help us. Oh, can you help us?*

The students' eyes shone as they scanned the faces that looked toward them from the hall. *My God! Where are the men?*

All these women and children. Old women!

Jesus, don't let them expect too much. How happy they seem that we're here! Smile back! God, we're actually here. In Ruleville!

Mrs. Williams beamed as she watched. "My," she thought, "wait till I tell Jim. All them beautiful youngsters! And wait till them scaird teachers see them!"

McLaurin took charge. From the moment he stood to quiet the applause he was in charge. His neat, compact body moved with agile assurance, and his voice throbbed with suppressed excitement. He slapped his strong hands loudly together, and his words rang like a summons through the packed room.

Go tell it on the mountain!

The audience took up the cadence and responded in a joyous surge of sound:

Over the hills and everywhere,
Go tell it on the mountains—
To let my people go!

Mrs. Williams boomed above the crowd:

Who's that yonder, dressed in white?
Let my people go!

My face was awash with sweat, and I abandoned my sketching to clap and listen. Charley Scattergood was rocking in rhythm, and he grinned as he caught my eye. His jaw had been broken by two Negroes who had jumped him as he walked through a Spokane slum, and it was still wired. Tears shone in his eyes, and he clapped as he sang.

"Who's that yonder dressed in black?" called a pert teen-age girl, double-timing her clap in an exuberant beat.

George Winter's head was thrown back. His eyes were closed, and he looked like a young Okie preacher shouting Gospel. I could hear his Midwest twang: "Must be the hypocrite turnin' back!"

LET MY PEOPLE GO!

Mac moved like an oiled cat. He built effortlessly from instruction to exhortation. The songs seemed to free him, and he winged his words intuitively, sensing the responses, building to his message naturally. "Tomorra we start signing folks up here in Ruleville. We're gonna knock on every door. And then we're goin' into Drew, and Shaw, even Indianola. Mr. Charlie's not goin' to like it, but we're goin'!"

A kind of inevitable logic worked through the text and the singing, and the "mass meeting" became a created whole. A unity of purpose and a sharing of aspiration grew almost visibly in the humid hothouse of Williams Chapel.

> *Ain't gonna let no-body turn me round,*
> *Turn me round,*
> *Turn me round,*
> *Ain't gonna let no-body turn me round,*
> *Keep on a'walkin', keep on a'talkin',*
> *Marchin' up to Freedom Land.*

The crowd moved up the aisles to the front of the chapel. The boys from the rear were among them, and the men who had sat tentatively on the side were now arranging themselves in the human chain. Arms crossed and hands reached out to neighbors.

"We Shall Overcome." The hands clasped and the anthem soared from the windows.

Two hundred yards away at the Billups Gas Station the men stood framed in the pool of light that shone flat and white over the pumps. They silently drank their Cokes and listened to the singing. A green pick-up truck spun its wheels in the dirt road and raced past the chapel. It wheeled with squealing tires onto Highway 41 and turned immediately into the Billups Station.

7

I drove into the narrow stretch of grass between Charlie Barber's house and the Williams'. Dale and Mrs. Williams climbed out of the car chattering and laughing. Together we climbed the back step and waited as Mr. Williams crossed in the yellow light and unlatched the screen.

"My, Jim! We had such a fine meetin'!" She heaved herself onto a kitchen chair as I poured four glasses of ice water from a chilled milk bottle from the refrigerator.

Mrs. Williams mopped her shining face. She looked sharply at Mr. Williams, and her eyes narrowed.

"Sharon all right?"

He shook his head. "Sound asleep." His forehead wrinkled and he sat down across the table, his eyes on Mrs. Williams.

"Charlie came by from next door after the news on the TV. He says three of the boys is missing. In Meridian."

From my pillow I could see just a thin rectangle of the front road and the first step of the house next door. The air was still warm and soft, and only the whir of the tree toads gentled the dark outside. I heard from what seemed a long distance a revved motor that ground its gears as it picked up speed. The noise was startling, and the drum of the tires could be heard clearly on the silent road. My tiny rectangle of street and step was suddenly blinding as the headlights caught it. A plummeting dark shape tore behind the whiteness and I realized it was a small pick-up truck. A second car squealed as it turned up our dirt road, and the gunned engine chattered as it spun its wheels. Once more the rectangle came alive, the light spraying across the torn step and the dusty stones. The two intruders moved to the end of the block, and I heard the motors slow and idle. Moments later they flew down the road once more, and the dark shapes swept past, the noise dipping and sliding into silence. I heard a whispering in the bedroom, and I knew I was not alone watching. And listening.

An incredible, rasping sound tore the shroud of my fatigue, and I was suddenly and completely awake. The room was awash with sunlight. Again the raw sound exploded under my window. I rolled on my belly and peered out. Four feet away the rooster was filling the air with an imperious trumpeting. I laughed, rolled on my back, and examined my watch. Five-fifteen. I shuddered, wondering if the rooster went off at that hour every morning. I reached for my notebook and my sketchpad. Remarkably, I felt fine. It was a pattern that was to continue for me the whole time I lived in the Delta. For an hour I busied myself with notes and drawings, and at six-thirty I swung my feet to the cool linoleum. I padded silently into the kitchen, carrying the green plastic pitcher from the lavatory. I filled it with the cold water from the single tap and took it into the tiny room which separated my bedroom from the kitchen. I slipped out of my pajamas and lay them across the top of the toilet tank. A shining, chipped porcelain basin hung from a hook over a small trestle table that was covered with a cracked and peeling oilcloth. I poured water into the basin, lathered my stubbled chin, and began to shave. A tiny ten-cent-store mirror was nailed to the wall, and I jockeyed to catch the reflection of my soaped whiskers. When I finished, I poured the water from the basin into the toilet and flushed it away. The plumbing rumbled and complained. Guiltily, I pressed my ear to the warped door, hoping I had not roused the whole household. I could hear soft voices in the other room, and the rattle of a frying pan in the kitchen. As I washed myself, the smell of frying bread filled the room. I could hear Sharon giggle outside my door. The garden outside the tiny window was full of dew and the air smelled good. I was humming when I went in to breakfast.

All the talk was of the missing workers. The news of the disappearance had flown through the quarter, and when I reached the chapel the kids were standing in knots around the steps.

"Gee, I had lunch with Andy last Friday."

"Which one was Mickey Schwerner? The kid with the beard?"

"Yeah. He had his wife with him at Oxford."

"They've been running a small community center in Meridian. Moses said at Oxford that they weren't having any real trouble there."

"It looks lousy. Not even a trace of the station wagon."

"Chaney's from Mississippi. He knows the score."

"That's why it looks lousy. He didn't get lost."

"What do you think, Mac?"

First news of the disappearance of James Chaney, Mickey Schwerner, and Andy Goodman

The questions stopped, and they all moved closer to listen. He stood on the first step, his hands deep in his pockets. His eyes behind the dark glasses were troubled, and he shook his head several times in the negative.

"They say in Jackson that the three of them were picked up for speeding, 'held for investigation,' and released at ten-thirty at night. That's the story they got from the Philadelphia sheriff." He shook his head vehemently and his face lifted. "Mickey Schwerner wouldn't have left a jail in Philadelphia at ten-thirty at night." Abruptly, he wheeled and went up the steps to the chapel. We followed him to the front and settled into the wooden seats. As I sketched the group, I counted. Eighteen.

Mac leaned against the pulpit, and his voice patiently spelled out the pattern of the days ahead. "The cars you heard moving through the quarter last night were vigilante cars." His finger pointed through the window. "They work out of the station over yonder. They don't know what we're doin' yet, so they're gonna keep movin' through the quarter to find out. So it's time we got our security operating. Dale, you move over to the Hamers' house today and set up communications. Three of our people are missing, probably they're dead. We've got to be careful, and we've got to keep in touch." He stopped, and the dark glasses swept the rows of seats. "From now on, call Gronemeier at the Hamers' when you get home at night. If you see cars and pick-up trucks movin' through the quarter, get their license numbers and pass them on to Dale. Stay away from windows if your light is on, and be careful. If there is any trouble, call in and we'll pass the word to the rest of the quarter. Dale will be in touch with Jackson, and he'll relay news in and out of Ruleville." He paused as a green pick-up truck moved slowly past the chapel. It stopped opposite my Chevvy as a white police truck appeared from the opposite direction. The bed of the police truck was a wire cage. The door swung open, and a large black and brown police dog paced back and forth on the tailgate. The two drivers spoke briefly, their faces turning toward my car and the windows of the chapel. The policeman noted my license number, and the two trucks moved slowly down the road.

"Look." McLaurin had turned from the window. We watched him closely as he folded his arms. "Mayor Dorrough, the police, the vigilantes—they all know you're here. They're worried sick about it." He slapped his hands sharply together and leaned toward the group. "Startin' at five o'clock we're gonna start working on getting these people in Ruleville to sign up to go to Indianola on Wednesday to try and register. And we've got to start now in getting them to register in the Freedom Democratic party. They're not allowed at a Democratic party caucus, so we've got to show the country that they'd register if they were given a fair chance. We'll need every name we can get when we go to the Democratic Convention next August." His voice hardened. "No police dog's gonna change that."

"Why five o'clock, Mac? Can't we start working in our neighborhoods now?" Gretchen's usually smiling face was intent, and she pulled absently at one of the thick braids of brown hair that touched her shoulder.

Mac shrugged. "Yeah, if you find anyone at home, go talk to 'em. But most of these people work from cain't to cain't, and they don't get back till five-fifteen." He saw the puzzled look, and grinned broadly. "'Cain't to cain't' means 'Cain't see in the mornin' cause it's too early, and cain't see at night cause it's too late.'" The smile disappeared. "The bus picks 'em up at Seal's grocery store at five o'clock. It leaves 'em off at Seal's at five o'clock. They make three dollars for twelve hours' work."

McLaurin sat down on the edge of the platform. "During the day some of you will be working on the Federal Projects part of the program, checking to see what government programs can be used to help these folks. Their average yearly income here in the Delta is six hundred dollars. Some of you will be working with Charley Scattergood and Mike Yarrow getting depositions from folks who have been intimidated by threats and

A view of white Ruleville from black Ruleville.

shootings. That's important, because if we can show a pattern exists to deprive folks of their right to vote, we can pass the information on to the Justice Department." He nodded toward a short, stocky boy wearing black-rimmed glasses. The boy was intently writing in a large loose-leaf notebook. "Jerry Tecklin will be doing research. His job will be to find out what the local power structure consists of. He'll be gathering information about the local plants, their contracts and suppliers. And he'll be finding out about the educational budgets and working conditions on the plantations. By the end of the summer we're all gonna know a lot more about Mississippi. We'll meet here every afternoon at four-thirty before we start canvassing."

I stepped out into the bright heat of the morning. Jim Corson, the young Methodist chaplain from Stanford, came down the steps with Jerry.

"I'm going into town and introduce myself to the mayor and the local Methodist minister. Jerry wants to get statements from the two banks in town and any chamber of commerce material. You want to come?"

The three of us began the ten-minute walk downtown. As we passed the gas station, three men stood in the office. Their eyes followed us as we crossed Route 41. Jerry fretted and muttered under his breath. "It's crazy. I really should go alone. Look, you guys, if I'm going to be able to get any information from these characters, I shouldn't be identified with you."

"Well, you do look awfully respectable in that jacket and all," said Jim. "Why don't you walk ten paces in front of us?"

Jerry threw him a fast, searching look.

"I mean it," said Jim, "we won't even pretend to know you."

Jerry had prepared for this assault on the local power structure. He had put on a tie and jacket, and in no stretch of the imagination could he be identified with the blue-jeaned, dusty students in the quarter. His serious face was already flushed with the sodden heat, and his collar was limp. He started to stride ahead, and suddenly stopped dead in his tracks and waited for us to catch up. He laughed and shook his head ruefully.

"This is nuts. They're going to know who I am by eleven o'clock this morning. So what in hell did I wear this tie for?"

We moved down the concrete sidewalks of white Ruleville. The road was paved and broad, curving prettily past cool, porched homes. The deeply shaded lawns stretched past plantings of fuschia and begonias and were tended and inviting. The tall elms and oaks laced fingers over the street, and the way to town was a leafy tunnel.

The tree-lined avenue ended abruptly as we entered the square in the center of town. A broad rectangular park was filled with old trees that threw welcome shadow on the benches and criss-crossing paths. But the streets and stores bounding the green island were pinned to the earth by a relentless sun that exposed every blemish.

We walked past a lot full of cultivators and trenching machinery and approached the row of stores that faced the park. The town looked still. Some women shoppers and their small children hugged the sides of buildings to escape the sun; farm trucks were parking in the center of the wide street, the drivers moving under their wide straw hats from hardware store to the café for coffee. Four elderly men sat on a shiny, worn yellow bench under the awning in front of the feed store. The light from the pavement reflected from the old eyes and the worn parchment skin. Their quiet chatting ceased as we approached, and we saw the closed look that we were to find every day in Mississippi.

Jim smiled and nodded as we passed. "Good morning!"

One of the old men instinctively started to answer, caught himself, and closed his mouth. He moved a chaw of tobacco from one side of his jaw to the other and gave a curt nod. The rest sat silent, their eyes cold and veiled. The three of us moved past the bank, a dry-goods store, a shoe store. We walked slowly, feeling the eyes from behind the counters and the plate-glass windows.

"Man," I breathed as we reached the corner. "I feel like Gary Cooper in *High Noon*."

Two Negro teen-agers crossed at the intersection. I had seen them at the meeting the night before, and they had obviously recognized us. I smiled as they approached. "Hi!" I called. Without breaking stride they moved past us. A fast smile and a murmured soft "Hi!" and they were gone. A white woman holding her little girl's hand stood watching intently in the drugstore doorway. As the Negroes moved up the block she turned, walking rapidly to her car, the child trotting to keep up. Her car passed us as it picked up speed. The child was unwrapping a lollipop, and she smiled. The mother's hands gripped the wheel, and her face was pale. She turned her glance from the road and looked directly at us. Her face was alive with hate and revulsion.

To our left, a short block away, was the small brick building that held the firehouse, the police station, the jail, and the chamber of commerce. Facing it was the red brick pile of the Methodist Church and Rectory. Along both sides were a scattering of nondescript stores, a small supermarket, a café.

To our right, the block that fronted on the park held the Rexall Drug Store, and the one shiny new building in town, Senator Eastland's bank. Handsome and contemporary, its quiet elegance shamed the rest of Ruleville's downtown, making the old buildings appear mean and poor. Inside the air-conditioned splendor of the bank was a small sign that said: "Senator Eastland's Office—Upstairs." Beneath it, all in capitals, "SMILE."

Straight through the intersection, the wide street we had traveled continued one block farther. On the left was an insurance office and the United States Post Office. On the right another grocery, and a silent tan-bricked building which said "Ruleville Hotel" over an absurdly ornate doorway. A small sign said "closed." (Talk in the quarter was that they had closed it to prevent integration problems arising from the "invasion.") At the Texaco Station the road narrowed again, leading south, eventually joining Route 41 beyond town. Facing the park on the far side were the sheds and tracks of the railroad. If one walked to the corner past the Ruleville bank and turned left, away from the park, he found a string of poor groceries run by Chinese and Negroes, a run-down café, and a tiny hamburger stand which was expanding through the efforts of its owner, Mr. King, into a large and going enterprise. He had already added a cement block shell, and the industry of his carpentry and electrification continued all summer. Beyond the small commercial area, a section of town populated by Negroes ranged along the railroad. This was "The Compress."

The white police truck was parked across from the Senator's bank. Both the cage and the cab were empty. I squinted in the glare and saw the policeman busily exercising the animal in the park. The dog raced through the speckled shade, its ears pricked to catch the commands of the policeman. I glanced at Corson and Jerry. Their eyes followed the dog as the policeman moved slowly back toward the truck. The dog sprang effortlessly to the tailgate and lay down panting in the cage. Jim touched my arm, and we turned down the street to the station house.

Mayor Dorrough leaned back in his chair, his cocoa-colored straw hat shoved back on his head. He was a florid, stocky man, beginning to run to fat. His face was large, and his eyes were calculating and cool behind his glasses. He looked like a comfortable small-town insurance salesman, which he was, and his voice rolled smooth and deep as he laced his fingers behind his neck.

"We don't expect any trouble here in Ruleville, and we're not goin' to stand for any bein' brought in. These outsiders and agitators aren't wanted here by anybody. Our Nigras are good people. We know them and they know us. There's nothing these beatnik kids can give them. They're happy folks, and they shore as hell don't want any trouble with the whites who they're goin' to have to get along with after these students go home. What are they doin' down here, anyway? Freedom Schools? Why, hell, we're spendin' more money on Nigra education in Sunflower County than on the white schools. Voter registration? Why, we've had Nigras voting in Ruleville for thirty-five years! The good Nigras who've voted all these years are fine people and we respect 'em. They know that these outside agitators are just stirring up trouble. Why, they're embarrassed that white girls are sleeping in the Nigra quarter! There's never any trouble from the Nigras here in Ruleville. And there's not going to be any. Last time we had trouble was two years ago when outside agitators came into town. They shot up

"We're down here to help you folks change things." Swarthmore student, Gretchen Schwarz, canvassing in Ruleville.

the Nigra homes in order to get money and publicity up North. Worked, too. All the northern papers were competin' to see who could vilify us the worst, and CBS did a documentary showin' these poor, mistreated darkies." He shoved back his chair. "I see by the register you signed that you're working for CBS, Mr. Sugarman." He stood up. "I hope you'll tell the truth about us. We're just folks down here."

I trailed behind, watching. The students paired off, working from house to house, block to block, through Jerusalem Quarter. They stood, awkwardly at first, seeking the right approach. The words came haltingly.

"Hello. Can I talk to you? For just a few minutes? Thanks. I'm Jeff Sacher."

"Hi. I'm Donna Howell. We're getting a group of people together to go register in Indianola Wednesday. Would you like to come with us?"

The Negroes sat in the cool shade of their tiny porches, or in rusted metal chairs under the tree in the yard. Many of them were still dusty from the fields, still wearing the bulky clothes they used to protect themselves from the flies, the snakes, and the sun. They followed the students' movement up the road. Their eyes narrowed as they cocked their heads to hear the talk in the neighbor's yard.

"We're down here to help you folks change things. If we can change them, a man won't work twelve hours for three dollars."

"Glad to meet you, Mrs. Turner. I'm George Winter. I live in a little town in California. Not much bigger than Ruleville."

"I'm John Harris, Mr. Woods. My home is in Birmingham. This is my friend, Len Edwards. He's learnin' to be a lawyer in Chicago. We'd like to talk to you about registering."

Hardly anyone signed that first afternoon. Yes, McLaurin had told them we were coming. A fine boy, McLaurin. But they'd have to see. Their eyes followed the police wagon as it edged slowly along the road. The dog stood on the tailgate, its legs braced. Its head jiggled with the movement of the truck.

They'd have to think about it.

8

I saw it begin in Mound Bayou. McLaurin, Jim Dann, and Jeff Sacher drove with me ten miles to the intersection in Cleveland. We turned north and continued the five miles to the edge of Mound Bayou. Mac pointed to the lights of a Negro café and said, "That's it." I nosed the Chevvy off the highway. Mac looked closely at the trucks parked in the area. "He's not here yet."

Lois waved from a table in the neon-lit bar. We slid into the booth with her. Lois said, "He'll be here in his truck by nine-thirty, Mac." With a warm smile she turned to the rest of us. "Welcome! Haven't seen you all since Oxford!"

"Good to see you again, Lois," said Jim. "Mac told me you're heading up the project in Cleveland. How's it going?"

"Slow. Too slow. We've got Shaw all set to take the people from the Freedom Schools when they get down, but we still don't have a place in Cleveland."

"What about Mound Bayou?" asked Jeff.

Lois shook her head disconsolately. "Amzie says we can crack it. I don't know. It's all colored in Mound Bayou, you know. And comfortable. In a lot of ways they feel they have it made, and why get involved. All that jazz." She sipped her beer and lit a cigarette. "But Amzie says we can do some good. He's called the first meeting for ten o'clock tonight. He ought to be along soon. Have a beer while you're waiting."

The red taillight of Amzie Moore's truck bounced and blinked in the darkness. My eye kept moving to the rearview mirror, for we had been winding through back-country dirt roads for fifteen minutes, and I was feeling prickly and exposed. Every side road was a hazard, and every approaching light could be a car of shotgun vigilantes. I peered nervously through the windshield as I saw the truck move up a grassy grade and stop. Silhouetted against the starry night was the looming bulk of the country church. It stood lonely and forlorn, its windows spilling a pale yellow light on the lawn. I pulled behind Moore and killed the headlights. As I opened the door the overhead light blazed on. McLaurin swore. "Close your door!" I pulled it closed and the light flicked off. "Man, you've

"They want to help us get started here, and that's why they're here tonight." Amzie Moore at the first meeting in Mound Bayou.

got to tape that switch down! You're a real target with that light over you. Get some electric tape tomorrow."

A tall heavy figure climbed from the truck and moved toward the door of the car. Amzie Moore took my hand and shook it warmly.

For years in the Delta, Moore had worked almost alone, an intrepid man who had made an unalterable decision. When he returned from the war, he decided it was time to stand up. The stubborn refusal to bend his head had changed his life and the lives of those who knew him. To the younger men in the Movement like James Jones and Charlie Cobb he was a pillar of strength. To Charles McLaurin he was almost a father. Moore ran a successful gasoline business, and he had fought the racists who

wanted to steal his franchise. Moore had taken them to court and won. His business interests were varied, but the generating force in his life was the Movement. His total commitment had ruined his marriage, leaving him alone in the fine house he had built in Cleveland.

Our small group sat in the center of the large hall. Ranged along the rear seats of the church were a handful of men, women, and children, perhaps thirty in all. They looked uncertainly about them as they watched Moore amble to the front of the congregation. He was well over six feet, and portly. A heavy neck supported his round, bald head. His voice was reedy, higher than one expected from so large a man. He gave a feeling of strength and gentleness that was altogether manly and attractive.

Jeff Sacher, student from Reed College.

"I want you good people in Mound Bayou to meet some of our friends who are working on voter registration in Ruleville. They want to help us get started here, and that's why they're here tonight. We can learn from them. Some of you know Charles McLaurin. I'll let him introduce the students to you."

As Mac introduced us, I watched the faces of the men and women in the rear. The psychological impact of these students from across America on the Mississippi Negro community was electric. They came into their lives as living testament that somewhere beyond the reach of the farthest White Citizens Council were people who knew—people who cared. There was an almost visible stiffening of resolve. What had always been impossible might, just might, be possible.

By the end of the hour real plans were being set in motion. Assignments were given. Goals were being discussed.

By the end of August two hundred people were attending mass meetings in Mound Bayou.

We stayed at Amzie's house that night. It had the feeling of bachelor quarters, the careless housekeeping of a man not yet used to living alone. Jeff and I opened the rumpled studio couch and were about to turn off the light when Moore came into the room. He laid a loaded Luger on the night table. "This is in case of emergency."

Jeff rose from the couch. "Amzie, we can't use it. If someone comes busting in here and finds us with a gun, we'll hurt the whole Summer Project."

Amzie picked up the Luger and slipped it in his pocket. "Just as you say," he said. "Good night."

As we slept in Cleveland that night, cars had sped past the Hamers' house. The racing wheels sent gravel and stones kicking across the bone-dry road. Dale came full awake in the parlor and moved instinctively to the darkened porch. He was still peering through the rusted screen into the black country night when the phone exploded in sound. Dennis Flanagan tumbled out of the house, hair tangled and eyes staring. Dale spoke quickly into the receiver. "Okay, I've got it. Stay away from the windows. I'll pass the word." Coca-Cola bottles had smashed into homes in the quarter. One had exploded against the battered roof of Len Edwards' car. When we arrived at the Hamers' next morning, chunks of green glass covered the hood and splinters of bottle sparkled on the dewy grass. Dale and Dennis had kept a long vigil, calling every home with a phone. For most of the students it had been a frightening and wakeful night. Dale came right to the point as they settled for the morning briefing.

"Starting tonight, we pull guard. Two each night. From now on."

9

I knew I was frightened as we approached Indianola. Our three-car caravan had moved down Route 41 at forty miles an hour. The Highway Patrol had raced past us, and I worried at what lay ahead. The nine Negro women from Ruleville chatted quietly as we turned off the highway and moved toward the center of the town. But the cars became silent as we parked across from the immense county courthouse. It was a tall, handsomely proportioned yellow brick building, and it filled the square. Its colonnaded entrances faced each of four streets with an imposing and austere mien. From its impressive cupola that crowned the soaring roof to the old white wooden columns, the place was an impressive symbol of authority. Clusters of whites were on the walks, and all heads were turned our way. I smiled at the women in my car. They sat in their churchgoing best, and their eyes were stead and determined. I took a deep breath and stepped out into the hot July sun. "Let's go, ladies," I said quietly.

As we mounted the sidewalk at the corner, I peered at the cluster of whites congregated at the steps leading to the courthouse. It was a great relief to recognize Chris Wren of *Look* Magazine and his photographer among them. They were reporters, and they smiled encouragingly as McLaurin and Donna led the women up the steps. Chris touched my arm and nodded toward the top of the stairs. At least a half-dozen deputies had suddenly materialized. Almost to a man they wore boots, narrow-brimmed straw hats, open sport shirts, badges, and conspicuous holsters. They stood in the shadow of the tall columns, hands carelessly resting on hips or cartridge belts. Some of them sucked on toothpicks, and the rest chewed gum or tobacco. They faces were hard and unsmiling. Chris whispered, "They look like they made up for the part!"

Sheriff Hollowell stepped from the shaded doorway and met McLaurin as he mounted the porch. He was a man of about forty, prematurely bald. He looked purposeful and intelligent, and remarkably cool. His shirt was short sleeved and unblemished by sweat, and he wore a neat dark tie. His eyes met Mac's. McLaurin nodded. "These folks are here from Ruleville. They want to apply to register."

Hollowell's eyes moved along the women on the steps, and his lips moved in distaste. He turned to McLaurin. "They can go in, two at a time. The rest will have to wait out here." His eyes moved and he squinted at the burning glare of the yard. "They can stay on the porch."

Donna led the women into the shade of the pillars, and they settled down on the stone railing to wait their turns. The deputies moved importantly and self-consciously up and down the stairs. The presence of photographers and reporters seemed to upset them. Their contemptuous stares moved from the press to Les Galt and Donna, who sat talking with the Ruleville women.

The sheriff had taken Mac aside and walked with him past the immense shiny-leafed magnolia across the lawn to the police chief's office. McLaurin walked with a bouncing assurance that he could not possibly

The heart of Indianola: county seat for Sunflower County, home of the
White Citizens Council.

have felt. I knew that he had been arrested and jailed four times right across the road in the Indianola jail.

I glanced out at the street. Crowds of whites ranged along the front of the stores. Cars edged down the street, the occupants whispering excitedly. Kids on bikes tore down the sidewalks, glancing furtively at the "mixers," wide-eyed. Two local Negroes moved swiftly across the intersection, never acknowledging the excitement. They disappeared quickly around the corner. Teen-aged boys leaned across the hood of my Chevvy, and I worriedly speculated about the long hours ahead. I moved up and down the walks, shooting pictures. A kind of anonymity seemed to go with the camera, and I could move about with less attention than when I was clearly identified with the students. It was only when I squatted on the grass, making sketches, that attention focused on me. Even the deputies would finally give way to their curiosity and sidle behind to watch me draw. The whispered talk behind me seemed to center on the "white girl, settin' with them niggers." Donna seemed oblivious, her tall, lithe figure moving easily back and forth on the porch, her long hair swinging at her shoulders.

The sun moved higher, and the July heat piled up in the square. McLaurin and the sheriff walked slowly back across the lawn. A convertible squealed around the corner, and six adolescents shouted a raucous chorus of profanity as the car sped down the block. Hoots and laughter from the watching whites followed it. Hallowell trotted up the stairs and spoke quietly to his first deputy, Parker, pointing at the receding car. The tall, beefy Parker sucked on his cigarette and frowned.

By noon, five of the women had been in to the registrar's office. The crowds of white thinned as some drifted down the side streets to the cafés and the bars. The registrar left for a long lunch, and some of the deputies left with him. The women from Ruleville sat sipping the Cokes that we fetched from the machine in the center hall of the courthouse. Their

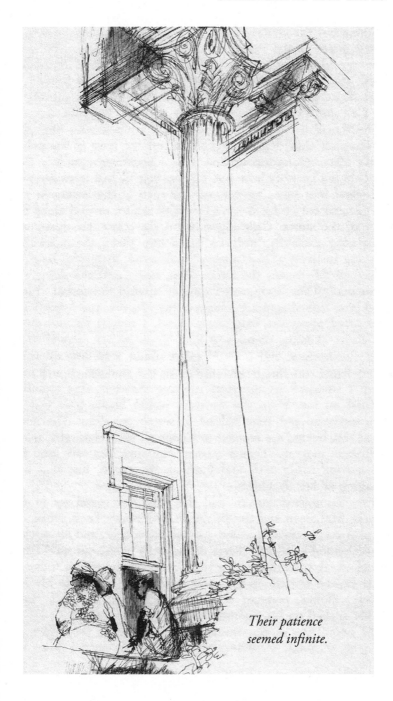

*Their patience
seemed infinite.*

patience seemed infinite. The square was almost deserted as the dizzying, suffocating midday heat paralyzed movement. The afternoon ground on. Two by two they made their way into the registrar's office. The clock on the bank seemed to creep. The sidewalks once more began to fill. The sullen quiet was shattered as the convertible careened around the corner. Once more the toughs shouted obscenities as they leaned from the speeding car. It circled the courthouse and pulled to the curb down the block. The young men spilled out, making their way up the walk to the courthouse.

Hallowell summoned Parker, and the two of them intercepted the group at the corner. The sheriff led the way across the street to the ugly, red stone jail. The boys looked bewildered, but Parker urged them ahead and they filed into the jail. For twenty minutes they were closeted with Hallowell at the jail. When they came out, they made straight for their car. Their faces were flushed and angry as the car passed, moving swiftly out of the square. Mac grinned. "He told me he didn't want any trouble!"

By four o'clock our nine women had finished the punishing ritual of voter application. They knew that now their names would run in the local papers for two weeks, alerting creditors, bosses, and landlords. They knew that when they returned one month hence that they would be told by the Man that they had not passed the test. And they knew that they would keep on coming until they were registered. I watched the women shuffling across the wide paved road to the cars. Their Sunday-best prints were soiled and wrinkled. Perspiration beaded their foreheads. The older women walked as though the broken shoes they had worn to "look nice in Indianola" were killing them. I opened the car door and held it as they filed in.

Waiting to apply to register to vote at the Indianola courthouse.

10

Mrs. Williams stood uncertainly in the doorway of my bedroom, blinking at the morning light through her round glasses. Her hair was still wrapped in a kerchief, and she clutched the ancient wrapper around her night clothes. Her face was gray. "They set the church on fire last night. I jes heard."

I swung my feet to the floor and grabbed my pants. "Put something on, Mrs. Williams, and we'll drive right over."

I glanced at my watch. Six-thirty! What in hell happened to the rooster?

Mrs. Williams carried Sharon and slid onto the front seat next to me. Mr. Williams rode silently in the rear. The news had shaken him badly, and his lips were moving silently as we approached Williams Chapel.

"Lord be praised—it's still there!" breathed Mrs. Williams. She stared through the dust-stained windshield. A fire bomb had exploded against the asbestos shingles beneath the eaves. The shingles were blackened where the gasoline had ignited and burned off. The bomb had fallen to the wooden steps and set fire to them. At two-thirty in the morning Mr. Hamer had heard the crash of the bottle and seen the flames. He had called the fire department, and in a very short time they had arrived and extinguished the fire. Dale had called all the students with phones and told them to show no lights and to stay inside.

Mr. and Mrs. Williams joined the crowd of Negros who stood staring at their scarred church. Their faces were shocked, and they spoke softly to each other. Their grief struggled with a sense of disbelief that anyone would set fire to their poor church. Their *church*! Mrs. Williams blinked like an owl through her cracked glasses. Sharon cuddled against her grandmother's ample shoulder, missing her morning bottle. She whined softly and Mrs. Williams gently patted her back. "Hush, now, Sharon." Her eyes

Spectator at the
Williams Chapel fire

Grief, shock, and disbelief that anyone would set their church on fire

remained on the black defacement of the chapel, and they were filled with
tears. "Hush. Or I'll get the switch."

Dale took me by the arm and led me to the side of the church. "Look
at these, but don't touch. The FBI is on the way out. Take some pictures
so we can send them to COFO headquarters." At intervals of six feet,
polyethylene bags full of gasoline had been laid alongside the chapel. If
the fire from the bomb had really started, the bags would have exploded
and the church would have been turned to ash.

I moved quickly around the church, recording the details of the arson. As I finished, a sedan parked directly in front of my car. The Negroes moved quietly aside as the four white men stepped from the car. They were chuckling at some private joke as they stepped across the ditch and moved through the crowd. I recognized Mayor Dorrough leading the two FBI agents and the fire chief toward the church entrance. He paused and pulled his cocoa straw hat closer over his eyes. His head bobbed in our direction as he noticed George, Dale, and me standing at the corner of the building. His words were clear and audible to the hushed folks watching. "They did it."

I stared at the short, runty figure. He's consistent, I thought. The other day he said the Negroes shot up their own homes. Today he says we set fire to our own church.

The four men huddled, speaking in low voices, and then the agents began to take notes and pictures. Chris Wren, who had driven with his photographer early that morning from Greenwood, approached the agents for a statement. The agents curtly refused the *Look* editor with a "no statement" and turned away. Moments later they followed Dorrough to the car and drove rapidly from the quarter. The sense of our isolation and vulnerability seemed to grow as their car disappeared in the shaded avenues of white Ruleville. I moved with the volunteers into the despondent crowd of Negroes, hoping to hearten them by our presence. The smell of gasoline was rank in the air, and my stomach felt sour and sick.

11

I had driven past the ugly cluster of houses and sheds on my first day in the Delta. Five miles before I reached Ruleville, the highway had made a wide swinging arc around the small mill town. A solitary, tall brick smokestack rose above the shed roofs of the warehouses and on its side,

Ruleville teen-agers canvassing in Drew.

in large capitals, it spelled DREW. It was visible across the table flatness of the Delta for miles before I entered the town.

By summer's end, we knew Drew. We knew it as soldiers know a town they have fought for. For us, Drew meant skirmishes and casualties—and, in the end, a kind of stalemate. Drew was a pocket of resistance that cost too much to take. We tried often, made limited gains, but our main efforts went elsewhere. Real breakthroughs came that summer in Shaw, in Ruleville, in Cleveland, in Mound Bayou, above all, in Indianola. Those were our hard won "Beginnings." For "beginnings" were all we were to know of victory in that long summer. In Drew, even the "beginning" eluded us. The evening of the day we took our people from Ruleville up the steps of the courthouse in Indianola, we made our first foray into Drew. Mac had brief us as we stretched out under the pecan tree in Mrs. Hamer's yard.

"We'll pull off the highway next to the school and park near the church. Go in twos, and fan out through the neighborhood on that side of the tracks. I'll work on the far side of town. At seven, sharp, we'll meet back at the cars and head out of town together. We don't want to be in Drew after dark."

At five the sun hung low in the west, flooding the dusty shacks and dilapidated bungalows of Drew with heat and burnished gold. The high, pale green sky framed a covey of pigeons as they wheeled across the rooftops, were lost momentarily in the brilliant glow of the western sky, and reappeared past the silhouetted mill, skittering down in a shimmer of wings somewhere in the quarter. The serenity of the Angelus hour was torn as we parked the three cars beside the church's vacant lot. Tension moved into the streets as we stepped from the cars. Mills and businesses in town had just closed, and a stream of workers drove down the dirt road toward the highway beyond. As they drove past, one could read the shock and indignation on their faces.

"Okay," said Mac briskly, "get goin'."

I slung my camera from my neck and trailed the volunteers as they worked through the neighborhood. Many of the workers, seeing us, had apparently abandoned all thought of driving directly home. Instead, they circled slowly through the quarter. When they would come alongside a student, they would lean from the window, spitting curses and abuse. We were their first "invaders," and they lost no time in reviling the volunteers as they made their way through the broken fences and up the dirt paths that led to the Negro homes. I noticed a pick-up truck that moved nervously through the roads, driven by the Drew Chief of Police. McLaurin had notified Sheriff Hollowell that we planned to go to Drew that night. Hallowell had indicated that peaceful canvassing would be tolerated in the county and had passed the word to the local police. The presence of the chief seemed to restrain the circling whites whose fury was building. At any moment, I felt, they would climb from their cars.

It was a dispiriting experience for our eager kids that night. The history of lynchings and violence in Drew was much too recent in the minds of the Negroes whom they approached. The Negroes would look nervously at the cars of the whites that kept passing the house, and drop their eyes as the volunteers would climb their porch step. Children were everywhere, but they held back, silent and watchful. A few followed my camera from a great distance, but when I would turn toward them, they would scatter, racing behind the shacks.

By six-thirty I started walking slowly back to the parked cars. A gas truck turned the corner as I approached. The driver viciously swung the wheel as I moved to the side of the road to let him pass. Startled, I leaped to the side, my camera swinging wildly, as the high fender grazed my thigh. The face in the cab was livid as he shouted "Sonuvabitch!" I was too astonished and breathless even to notice his license number.

The students started to congregate as the minutes dragged slowly past. The stream of cars continued to edge by us. Suddenly, a green Plymouth stopped dead in the middle of the road opposite our cars, blocking the way from the quarter to the highway. In moments a half-dozen cars were lined along the road. I glanced nervously at my watch. Six forty-five. The cars idled their motors, and the angry faces stared through the settling cloud of dust. A woman sat impassively as her husband leaned from the window of the green Plymouth.

"You chicken bastards!" His voice cut the silence, a ragged, grating yell. "You goddam nigger-loving sonsuvbitches! What are you doin' down here?" The southern singsong cadence of his speech rose, and his face was flushed and furious. "I said, what are you white niggers doin' down here?"

The students stood silent, turning from the strident rantings of the infuriated man or shifting nervously, watching with mounting alarm as the string of halted cars grew longer. I eyed the corner, praying that Mac would arrive early so we could leave before the fury of the overheated cars spilled into naked violence. The face of the woman in the Plymouth was pale and shut as her husband screamed insults and epithets in a torrent of abuse. Larry Archibald reddened, and he stepped from the crowd of students. He was a gangling, lanky, suddenly tall youngster. A tentative, struggling, red moustache made him seem even younger. He looked, with his horn-rimmed glasses, like a musical-comedy sophomore. His boyish voice rose in the sudden silence. "But, sir! We're just down here to help these people to register to vote!"

I saw the raging man in the Plymouth reach for the door handle as his incredulous face turned toward Larry. "You're what?" he exploded.

I reached quickly for Larry's arm. "Cool it, Larry! Shut up!"

Larry looked suddenly flustered and hurt. "But...." He stopped. Abruptly, he turned away from the car. I held my breath, for we all sensed that the moment the first car door opened, every car would empty. But the man's rage had spent itself in obscenity. With a growl of tires in the dirt, the Plymouth lurched forward and moved down the road. The line of cars raced their motors and edged past, the faces of the drivers unforgiving, staring.

*A voter registration team
at work in Drew.*

With relief we saw McLaurin turn the corner at the church. The mask of his sunglasses hid his eyes from the hating faces in the cars. He moved jauntily down the walk. "Time to move out," he sang, and climbed into the front seat of my Chevvy. I wiped the sweat from my eyes and glanced sideways at Mac as I turned the key in the ignition. He was studying the crowd of Negroes on the far edge of the dirt road. His eyes brushed past the children who were now edging close around our cars and lingered on the knots of men and women who stood watching. Now that the last white car had moved to the highway, the Negroes appeared on porches and along the short dusty hedges that edged the street. He smiled broadly and waved gaily. His voice rose as we started down the road. "We'll be back!"

The meeting that night was taut. Disappointment at the meager results in Drew combined with a growing awareness of the explosive violence which lurked just below the surface of our lives in the Delta. The thrown bottles, the fired church, the circling vigilante trucks, the news from Philadelphia that a burned-out station wagon had been found but that the boys were still missing, all added strain to the meeting at Williams Chapel. I studied the youngsters as they made their way into the steaming little church. The dust and fatigue of the Delta was subtly changing their young faces. There was less of the quick laughter one heard at Oxford. A new intensity, a kind of honed-down quality, was evident in their eyes as they looked about them. The self-conscious attempts to ingratiate themselves to the natives of Ruleville that one saw at the beginning was no longer evident. In its place was a growing sense of self and of purpose which was at once respectful and comfortable. The Negroes were beginning to see the students as people they knew and trusted. The students' camaraderie with the Negroes was as easy as it was inevitable. Cut off from the white world they knew, they were finding comfort and warmth within

George Winter, Ione, California, and a potential voter in Drew, Mississippi.

the Negro community. The symbolic identification with the aspirations of the Negro that had brought these youngsters to Mississippi was now being made real by a sharing of fears and disappointments, and the chastening effects of day-by-day life in the Delta. The church meetings which had meant so much to the Negro since slavery became now a real fount of strength to the students as well.

The meeting that night was like so many others. It combined the pragmatic approach of a political clubhouse with the throbbing responsiveness of a revival. Echoes of "Yes!" "Yes!" and "Amen" interspersed the speeches. The "Movement" seemed to have become the marvelous reason for losing doubt, licking fear, becoming resolute. "Stand up! Stand UP! Don't be moved—we shall overcome—we shall, we shall!" My eyes teared as I watched the elderly Negros in the chapel. They built their shrine with their religious faith, summoning their courage by singing the spirituals which had been reshaped to the great design of the "Movement." River Jordan is segregation—and they're gonna cross, gonna cross. Heaven is freedom, and hell is Mr. Charlie and the police dogs. "Ain't gonna let nobody turn me round...." Saul and David marched with Emmett Till and Medgar Evers and all those who have been "'buked and scorned." All had to be willing to pay with pain for a ticket on the "Freedom Train."

Charlie McLaurin led the meeting with a fervor that seemed to have grown from the frustrations of the afternoon. He sensed the disappointment felt by the workers, and he instinctively reached for a way to make them understand self-doubting. "I want you to know how I got in the Movement. It didn't happen all at once. It didn't happen easy. I didn't just decide, and that's that. Uh-uh. No, sir. Let me tell you. It started for me when some white guys entered the Negro community in Jackson where I lived. They took a piece of wire and looped it around the neck of a ten-year-old girl and drug her down the street. They hurt her bad. She was the niece of a buddy of mine. I was part of a group that used to fool around together, play football. And the night they did that to the little girl, we decided to go out and find the persons who had hurt her."

The damp heat of the church was soaking his shirt as he spoke to the silent crowd.

"We were trying to map out some strategy about what we were going to do to retaliate, and that's when Reverend Bevel came and stood up on the car to speak to us. He said that we were brave in the dark, we were going to shoot somebody in the dark or hit somebody on the head in the dark. And he challenged us to do something in the light, if we had the guts. He said we could take that energy and go to the bus station and buy a ticket in the main waiting room which was on the white side. He said we could take that energy and go buy a Coke in the restaurant where it was supposed to be open to the public. That was in 1961, when the Freedom Rides were just about to come into Mississippi. I went with my buddies downtown in Jackson and right up to the bus station. They went in. I didn't."

The fans had stopped moving in the hands of the women. I watched Mrs. Williams as she strained forward, bending her head not to miss a word.

McLaurin lifted his chin and said in a very clear voice that carried to the back of the church: "I didn't have the courage. Not then. Not the nest day either. Jim Jones and the other six went in and they got arrested. Jim went to Parchman Penitentiary for fifty-six days. Finally, I got the courage to walk up to the white window in that station in Jackson. And I've been in the Movement ever since."

McLaurin stood before us, sharing our fear and our doubts, making us bigger by the generosity of his spirit. The meeting was a great, surging success.

12

My yellow car with the Tennessee plates had become a familiar sight in the Delta. I knew it and worried about it. The Chevvy could be spotted so easily that I longed for a less conspicuous vehicle. It had become an indispensable part of the Ruleville operation, and I feared that the bright color would compromise its usefulness. Certainly the police and the restless

Watchers.

vigilante trucks could quickly know when we were moving in and out of Ruleville. In the brief span of time I had been there, I had transported students to Greenville to fill a picket line at the Federal building, driving voting registrants to Indianola, McLaurin to Cleveland and Mound Bayou, and twice carried volunteers into Drew. A score of times I had moved through white Ruleville, past the white public pool, the white high school, the police station. Each time I was scrutinized. Often I was followed by a watchful car or truck. By week's end, the constant scanning of the rearview mirror, the cautious measuring of side-road entrances, the gnawing uncertainty of the car passing and the truck approaching had made me decide to trade in the yellow car. I would have to drive south to the capital.

Dale accompanied me as I headed for Jackson, and the sense of adventure mounted as we moved for the first time out of the Delta. The fecund flatness slowly undulated as I pushed the Chevvy south and east. The encircling round of sky and plantation, the wheeling endless green ribbons of cotton plants were subtly transformed as the land began to rise and dip. For the first time groves of trees rose to challenge the vast horizon. As the car raced through unfamiliar patterns of shade, I caught flashes of light among the black stands of cypress as the following sun shot reflections in the swamp water. The highway south of Yazoo became an ascending and plunging track that scissored its way through a strange, viridian world. For miles the land had surrendered to a climbing, smothering vine which shone like ivy. Ground, shrubs, trees, rocks—all were enveloped and transformed. The shapes were myriad, ever-changing in the harsh, challenging morning light.

The thrum of the wheels, the soft air spilling through the car, the golden light of the Mississippi morning combined to bring a relaxed sense of holiday. We reveled in the release we felt at leaving behind our little garrison in Ruleville.

Jackson was a bustling, building shiny city of the New South. The new construction disappeared as I drove into the Negro wards. I dropped Dale at COFO headquarters, an innocuous storefront, its blown-out windows boarded up and anonymous. A Jackson police car parked across the wide avenue and watched me as I nosed into the traffic and headed for the Hertz office.

From the moment the young Mississippian greeted me with a pleasant, soft drawl I knew it was going to be awkward. I could not simply say, "I'd like to trade in my conspicuous yellow car with Tennessee plates for a dull car with Mississippi markers." Instead, I said, "I'd like to trade in my two-door Chevvy for a four-door sedan, please." He smiled agreeably.

"Are you with one of the newspapers?" he asked.

I shook my head. "No. But I'm doing some work for CBS and I'd find a four-door car more convenient. Equipment, you know."

He nodded. "Of course. Well, you're lucky. There are so many press folk down here now that there's rarely a car free. But in two hours I'm expectin' a car from the airport." He examined a yellow sheet on his desk and smiled at me. "Air-conditioned, too!"

"Fine! Thank you. I'll be back after lunch."

I dined in a small Negro bar and grill with lawyers who were volunteering their services to COFO for the Summer Project. They were bursting with humor and exasperation at the exotic character of Mississippi justice. They all looked exhilarated and tired.

"The toughest part is trying to cover so much territory," Alan Nevas, a young lawyer from Connecticut, in black horn-rimmed glasses, said thoughtfully. "But, hell, if the local sheriff expects a lawyer is going to be at the jail bright and early in the morning to interview his prisoner, the chances are a lot better that the prisoner is going to be in one piece. We've got to be there. And these deputies and jailers have got to get to expect us."

Another nodded assent. "They better had." He lit a cigarette and looked at me. "In places like the Delta there's damn little law if there are no lawyers." He laughed and continued. "There's damn little law *with* lawyers!"

Nevas nodded and turned to me. "Did you know that until we all came here to work this summer there was not a single white lawyer who would take a civil rights case in Mississippi?" He shook his head in wonder. "Not one."

Marion Wright, a pretty young Negro woman from New York who had decided to establish a permanent practice in the state, nodded. "And the three Negro lawyers in the state," she said, "are here in Jackson."

I picked up Dale and drove directly to the Hertz office. The young man behind the counter was all smiles. "Yessir! It came in just a few minutes ago. They're servicin' it and cleanin' it up for you." He handed me the forms to sign. I filled out the forms, and as I handed them across the desk I observed casually:

"I suppose the car has Mississippi license plates?"

He looked surprised. "Oh, yessir. It does, indeed! Four-door. Air-conditioned. I'm right sure you'll like it."

I heard a motor start in the garage and my new car backed to the office door. I stared and swallowed. A new Chevvy—four-door, air-conditioned, Mississippi plates—and red as a fire engine!

13

I sat on the Hamers' steps with Jerry Tecklin and Len Edwards. We saw a dusty car move swiftly into the quarter and watched as it pulled up abruptly in front of the Hamers' path. Two Negro men leaned into the rear seat and assisted a stricken woman from the car. She moved with great difficulty and seemed dazed. Wisps of gray hair clung to her damp forehead, and her mouth moved silently. Her breathing was labored, and her bosom heaved as if she were gasping for air. Donna Howell ran down the steps from the porch and tenderly helped the woman up the steps and into the parlor. I recognized one of the men from meetings at the chapel. He turned his face toward me, and I saw tears standing in his eyes.

His voice was low and husky. "She's Isaiah Taylor's mother." His eyes held mine. "Haven't you heard? Isaiah was shot to death late yesterday afternoon. In Doddsville. 'Bout five miles from here."

I shook my head. "No. We didn't hear. But who shot him?"

His voice was toneless. "A state highway patrolman."

Dale sat motionless by the woman's side, asking only the questions that were essential. Her story was a ragged, almost indecipherable patchwork. News of the killing had come to her not from the police but from a neighbor. She had rushed, frantic with grief and disbelief, to the Doddsville Police Station. The old woman's face twisted and crumbled. "The Man said…." Her voice broke, and her shoulders wrenched as a sob moved in her throat. Her eyes stared, seeing the station. "The Man said … 'Get this hollerin' woman outta here.'" Her laced hands covered her mouth, and the tears ran heedless down her cheeks. Donna wept as she embraced the old woman. Mrs. Taylor's voice was muffled with grief as her head shook against Donna's breast. "They never even let me see my boy."

McLaurin had stayed on the porch, questioning the two men who had brought Mrs. Taylor. I made my way silently from the room and stood beside him. "What should we do, Mac?"

"Go right to Indianola and get a statement from the sheriff. These fellows will take Mrs. Taylor home and make arrangements for the funeral."

As we drove from Ruleville, McLaurin pointed to the last house before the great sweep of cotton fields began. A torn screen door hung agape, and the dark gray hulk of unpainted wood stood forlorn in the sunshine.

"That's Mrs. Taylor's house. She lived there with Isaiah. He was mental, been in the hospital three times. Last time he was released was just over a year ago. A harmless guy, though. Never gave anybody a hard time. He was kind of a local character. Everybody knew Isaiah. He'd stand right near the highway, long about here, and wave at the cars as they'd pass. Every cop in Sunflower County knew him. He'd lived here all his life. Must have been about thirty-three or -four."

Dale was huddled in the crowded back seat, writing in his notebook, getting the facts for a report to Jackson. "What did you find out about the shooting, Mac?"

McLaurin frowned. "Not too much. According to the neighbors, the highway patrolman was driving with an off-duty policeman from another district. They say that the patrol car passed Isaiah, went a little way up the road, and made a U turn and came back. The two policemen got out of the car and went up to Isaiah to question him. According to the neighbors, the off-duty cop knocked Taylor down. They say that when he got up, he moved toward the highway patrolman. The patrolman fired two shots into the dirt as a warning. When Isaiah kept moving, he shot him dead." McLaurin was silent for a long minute. When he spoke again his voice was bitter. "There won't be any witnesses for Isaiah. There never are. The Negroes who saw what happened won't dare to testify. Not in Doddsville. And the whites will have their own story...." Again he was silent.

The car was skirting part of Senator Eastland's plantation. McLaurin's voice cut the silence in the car. "A Negro's life in Sunflower County isn't worth *that*." His hand rose in a fist. He unclenched the fingers and pressed the thumb and second finger together. They strained and snapped—like a shot.

Sheriff Hollowell was civil, even hospitable. He met us in the hall of the deserted courthouse. "Saturday," he explained. "Everybody's gone fishin'." He led the way down the shadowy hall. "Come on in my office. It's cooler."

For an hour the sheriff answered our questions. Dale took the statement meticulously, reading back what the sheriff had said for confirmation. Hallowell's bald head would nod agreement. At his elbow sat Deputy Parker, his beefy face impassive. He was finding it harder to be polite than the sheriff, and the fact that she shared the table with two Negroes, McLaurin and Harris, rankled. His jaw cradled a wad of gum, and he sat silent for the whole hour.

The sheriff's version of the killing differed significantly from the one we had heard earlier. According to the notes in front of him, Taylor had been stopped by the Highway Patrol because they wanted to question him. Some convicts had escaped from the county farm in Moorhead some days prior, and the officers were attempting to ascertain if this man was one of them. Taylor was reported to have refused to stop, had kept walking away from the officers and cursed them. The officers had then put him under arrest, at which time Taylor was reputed to have slashed at the officers with a knife. The highway patrolman had then fired two warning shots into the ground. Taylor drew back his arm and threw the knife as the arresting officer fired, struck, and killed him. The knife was supposed to have glanced off the scalp of the officer and sailed an additional fifty feet. The officer had sustained a minor abrasion.

Len Edwards leaned toward the sheriff. "Where is the knife, sheriff?"

"It's at the Mississippi State Highway Patrol laboratory," he answered coolly.

"Did you find the knife when you went to the scene of the shooting?" asked Len.

"Well, not just then. The knife landed in a cotton field and we didn't find it just then."

"When was the knife found, sheriff?" Len's voice was dry.

"Two hours later," said Hollowell, shortly. He leaned back in his chair and laced his fingers behind his neck. "All these facts were brought out at the hearing in Doddsville that took place at ten-thirty this morning."

McLaurin hunched his shoulders and leaned his elbows on the table. His voice was even and quiet. "Were there any witnesses at the hearing this morning?"

Hollowell nodded. "A number of them. People who worked at the Doddsville gas station. One of them was a Negro."

Mississippi policemen.

"Could we see the officer who shot Taylor?" asked Len. "The one whose scalp was slightly injured?"

Sheriff Hallowell gathered his papers and shoved back his chair. "That's impossible. You see, the presiding justice at the hearing in Doddsville acquitted him—'justifiable homicide.' He's back on duty."

It was a beautiful, hot Sunday—a carbon of almost every morning that summer. The complaining rooster nudged me to wakefulness, and I lay still, my eyes closed to the brightness that flooded my room. The now familiar sounds of the household were predictable and comforting. The lazy drip of the water as it plopped into the kitchen pail, the soft throaty rumble of Mrs. Williams' laugh as she joshed with Sharon, the sweet murmur of Mr. Williams' gentle replies, the coos and giggles of Sharon as she played peekaboo with the sheet. The Williams seemed to find an endless vein of conversation to amuse themselves with. At the moment it was small gossip about the neighbors' scrap that had livened the Saturday night in the neighborhood. The "scaird schoolteacher" had raised sand with her husband Charley when he came rolling home. "My," laughed Mrs. Williams, "that Charley was *full*." Both Mr. and Mrs. Williams had a lively and continuing alertness to the breaking news, and a vast and charming miscellany of interest which included the "Movement," cookery, the "old days," Sharon, Mississippi, sharecropping, their children, tenant farming, and the Holy Christ Gospel Church.

Mr. Williams left early for the church. Being an elder, his responsibilities included laying out the sacramental wine and biscuits before the arrival of the first congregants. After breakfast, I accompanied a shiny and brushed Mrs. Williams and a pink and bonneted Sharon to services. My cotton jacket felt heavy in the sodden heat, but I felt that decorum demanded my "Sunday-best" as well. Mrs. Williams deposited Sharon in the arms of an ample woman friend who was seated with the adults in the front of the room, and made her way to the rear, shooing children ahead of her like a mother hen. "Come on, now! It's time for Bible class!"

The children, boys and girls from five to fifteen, scrambled to the rear, sliding into facing wooden benches. Mrs. Williams distributed small Baptist booklets and took her place behind the benches, her girth a commanding presence to the assembled children. Her mock severity melted as she saw me listening and watching. Her wise eyes twinkled behind the cracked glasses. "This morning we're goin' to read why we welcomes the stranger at our gates."

Mr. Williams made a fine appearance as he moved with dignity to the altar. He read the opening prayer in his old man's voice, carefully enunciating each word. In his striped flannel pants, neatly pressed white short-

"This morning we're goin' to read why we welcomes the strangers at our gates."

sleeve shirt, and slim tie held by a clasp, the white-moustached spare figure was every inch an elder of the church.

The congregation had no paid preacher, so the lesson was taught and the singing led by Mr. King, who owned the small café in town. He was a handsome and vital man of thirty-eight. Armed with an intimate familiarity of the Gospel, he led the adults in a dialogue on Christian duty and Christian love. He was a sterling teacher, full to the brim with a surging enthusiasm for his subject. While preaching, he appeared intent and concerned, but a radiant smile would suddenly illuminate his countenance, and the congregation would be warmed and moved to a sighing and fervant response. "Yes. Oh, yes!" During a detailed reading of Scriptures, he patiently enumerated all that the good Christian should seek in Christian love. He concluded by tossing his head, his eyes kindled and laughing. "Love," he said with fervor, "is simply great!"

Dale joined us for Sunday dinner in the Williams' kitchen. He told us that a number of the volunteers had accompanied their host families to one or another of the five small Negro congregations.

"Did Len Edwards go to the white Methodist Church in Ruleville with Jim Corson?" I asked. The Methodist chaplain had told me that he intended to go to services on Sunday. The day we had walked to town, he had notified the local minister of his intentions. Len had hoped to join him.

Dale looked around the table. "Reverend Corson had visitors early this morning. Mayor Dorrough drove out to visit Jim, accompanied by one of the Ruleville aldermen. Jim and Len were about to drive to church. The Mayor came to their door and announced, "Corson, you're livin' with Nigras, so you go to the Nigra church—and stay away from ours.""

Mrs. Williams shook her head and clucked her tongue. "Imagine that. Jus' imagine that! A Methodis' minister bein' told he cain't come to a Methodis' church." She shook her head and rose to clear the table. She turned at the stove and grinned. "Does sound like Mayor Dorrough, though!"

14

The disappearance of Chaney, Goodman, and Schwerner haunted the COFO leadership. Basic re-evaluations of security had to be made, and a meeting of the Project heads was planned. Pending decisions from that meeting in Jackson, all voter registration activity was to be confined to towns where our workers lived. The students fretted at the order. Jim Dann spoke out angrily, and he seemed to mirror the feelings of the group. "We've started something in Drew. We've promised them that we'll be back. Some of them have even come down to our meetings here. What the hell do we tell them? That we'd like to work in their town, but Jackson says we can't because it's too dangerous?"

McLaurin nodded sympathetically. "They expect us back in Drew, and we'll be goin' back. But first we've got to have the meeting with Forman and Moses and the rest in Jackson. Meanwhile, we can help Mrs. Hamer get the Freedom School people settled when they arrive, and they're going to need a lot of help getting the school and library set up." He looked at Jim Dann and grinned. "Mann, we'll be going back to Drew. And Shaw. And Cleveland." He looked dreamily out the window. "And one day soon we're going to be going into Indianola."

A new burst of energy moved into the quarter with the arrival of the buoyant newcomers. They climbed from the bus, creased and tired, but full of a zest for the work ahead. Shaw and Cleveland were not yet ready to set up their schools and centers, so Ruleville became the temporary home for about twenty of the boys and girls who would move on in the next week. For the first time there were more girls than boys. I watched as Scattergood, Dann, Winter, and the rest of the "veterans" jumped to help get them settled. The festive air of a college "week end" moved into the dusty quarter. Mrs. Hamer trudged up the path to her house, carrying her suitcase. She turned at the step and watched the excited chattering. Her eyes moved to the gas station near the highway. A tight knot of whites were standing on the pavement near the pumps, watching. She frowned and turned to the porch. She dropped her valise and opened her arms as her daughter Virgie rushed happily to embrace her. "Mama! Mama, you been away so long!"

Alongside the highway that divided Jerusalem and Sanctified Quarters stood an ancient house of gray, unpainted wood. It stood on the corner of a dirt road that met the highway. Behind it stretched a large open lot

A pile for "Language." A pile for "History." A pile for "crud."

which belonged to the Sanctified Church, the peeling, white clapboard building that perched on the next corner within the quarter. Two empty rooms, a hallway, and an attic of the gray house had been rented by COFO from an absentee Negro landlord. I stood surveying the wreck, appalled at the state of hopeless disrepair. Grinding, relentless poverty had stamped it indelibly, and the generations of families who had lived there had been unable to bring anything to the old frame house. It stood dispirited and broken, occupied now by two old women who lived in the rooms facing the highway. I tramped through the building, slapping at the swarms of mosquitoes that rose as I entered. Rotted bedding, blackened and cracked windows, and walls that were stained and mildewed from years of seeping rain and snow spoke a wordless, broken language of despair. I was sickened by it, and made my way quickly back to the sagging porch.

One of the new girls was tying a bandana around her hair, and she saw my look of disgust as I came out of the house. She smiled and stooped to grab a bucket of suds. "Don't you know that a community center is a state of mind?" she said lightly, and disappeared through the torn screen door.

The assault on that incredible relic of a house could only have been mounted by the energy of the dedicated young. They invaded the musty interiors with brooms and mops, pails and soap, and emerged bearing the old accumulated filth. A pile of bedsprings and rags, old bottles and broken chairs rose in a corner of the yard, an odorous monument of neglect. Brigades of buckets swabbed out the grimy corners and light moved into the rooms through shining windows. The kids' laughter mingled with the chatter of broken glass being swept, and raucous hollers of "Who swiped my 'Tide'?" and "Jesus, just look at that toilet!" The packed dirt of the yard was buried beneath hundreds of cartons of books that had accompanied the teachers from Oxford and the soles of sneakers and moccasins as the youngsters swarmed about their loot. They tore open the corrugated boxes, yelling delightedly as they would discover a treasured book from their childhood or a reference volume that had saved their life on a college thesis. These were people who knew and loved books, and their happiness shone as they tore with relish into the mountains of pulp. Stacks of books began to build, "History," "Reference," "Language." A large number were being consigned to a corner of the yard, and I sought in vain to find a scrawled cardboard sign identifying them. A pretty girl from Oberlin College, Linda Davis, was assembling neat piles of children's books, and I pointed to the large mound of books accumulating in the corner. "What are those?" I asked. She laughed, and her ponytail bounced. "We've labeled that pile 'crud'!"

Amid the sweaty excitement was a contagious enthusiasm that spread

"Don't you know that a community center is a state of mind?"

through the quarter. Whispering groups of Negro children had gathered on the edge of the lawn during the morning. By afternoon they were beginning to leaf through some of the scattered volumes, encouraged by the smiles of the sweating students. A Negro man backed his battered truck into the yard and began loading the piles of debris. Local boys moved to help him as others started a small fire in the empty lot to burn away the debris. Slowly the ground began to clear, leaving only the confusion of the piles and cartons of books. Negro women began to appear, kerchiefs tied around their heads. Shyly, they moved up the creaking steps bearing pails and brooms.

Les Galt was stripped to the waist, and his sunburned back glistened in the sunlight. He kidded with the local boys as he organized a search for lumber. The kids were laughing and excited as they fanned out through Sanctified and Jerusalem quarters. For hours they scoured the poor back yards and empty lots. Slowly, a pile of splintered remnants began to rise as the boys came trotting back with their finds, pride and pleasure in their grinning faces. Les wiped sweat from his face and flicked his long hair from his eyes. He grimaced as he looked around the chaotic lawn.

"My God," he groaned. "Where are we going to find enough shelves for all these books, Fred?"

The sandy, moustached youngster who was straining to remove the nails and spikes from the wood remnants threw down a piece of scrap lumber in disgust. He was a carpenter from the West Coast, and he was used to working with clean, virginal strips of wood that smelled of the sawmill. His professional tool box sat shining amid the welter of tired scraps.

"The only lumber I've seen that could make respectable shelves," he said slowly, "is standing over there." His eyes moved to the outhouse and lingered lovingly on the seven-foot vertical shanks that rose to the pitched roof.

Communications Center in a Ruleville farmhouse.

Les turned to me. "They don't use that anymore, do they? Isn't there a toilet in that room off the end of the porch?"

I nodded.

Wordlessly, the two moved with crowbar and claw hammer to the lonely structure at the rear of the lawn. Three of the local boys ran to assist, giggling as they helped the two young men tilt the privy. With a groan of wood and a yell of triumph, the tiny house was felled. Like a stricken beast, she submitted to the carrion birds that descended upon her. Swiftly, the lumber was stripped from her carcass, leaving only a skeleton of ancient two-by-fours and a solitary box.

Lucia Guest, the only white southern teacher in the Freedom School, watched the conquest with amusement. She was a North Carolina girl, and her speech was a pretty echo of the southern mountains.

"I've got a great idea how to use that great pile of 'crud,'" she mused. "Now that we've got shelves, we'll need shelf supports. And hardware costs." She ran into the house and came back, carrying an enormous roll of rose-colored shelf paper. She tore off a four-foot section of paper and laid it flat on the ground. Quickly, she packaged a dozen books from the pile of rejects, scotch-taping the folded sheets into a neat bundle.

"With a package at each end of the shelves, you can support the next shelf above it." Happily, she reached for the next pile of "crud."

By mid-afternoon the scabrous walls and ceilings were being hidden with rolls of the brightly colored shelf paper, and by late afternoon the house stood transformed. Neat piles of books were arranged along the walls of the hall and the two rooms, awaiting the shelves, and the attic groaned with hundreds of books that would go eventually to other Freedom Schools as they opened. Packages of books to be used as supports were filling one end of the porch. The students and their Freedom School smelled from Lysol, soap, and mosquito spray.

I walked across the lawn to my car and looked at the house. The sky had darkened suddenly, and students raced toward the porch carrying the last sorted piles of books from the yard. A corkscrew of light ripped the endless Delta sky, and a rolling bellow of sound swept across the cotton fields. The sky to the south was a yellowish lead, and an enormous thunderhead raced toward the northeast. The students dragged and hauled the cartons from the porch into the hallway as the first fat drops of rain sprinkled the dust of the road with tiny explosions.

15

The sky rumbled and cracked. A torrent of cool water blinded the eye and a pounding, drenching flood swept into the caked fields and the dusty roads of the Negro quarter. It filled the alleys between the rows of cotton and puddled every rut in a twinkling. The water beat a loud staccato on the corrugated iron roofs, and a thousand frigid streams spilled on the heads of folks rushing for cover. I stripped off my shirt and reveled in the clean smell and the wet chill of the storm. Like a kid splashing in a puddle, I gave myself to the shower, and joyously drenched my pants and socks and shoes. I raced to the Williams', tore off my sodden clothes, and ran outside with a bar of soap!

The last rags of cloud were flying toward the north, and the dusk smelled sweet after the rain. Drops fell to the lank lawn from the shining leaves of the pecan tree, splashing in tiny plops on the abandoned wooden bench near the trunk. Fannie Lou Hamer stood on the porch and held the old flowered wrapper closed with a tight fist. The two cars moved slowly through the puddles of East Lafayette Street and turned at the corner. "They're goin' past the center again," she thought. Her eyes moved from the cars to her husband. "Pap," she said in a low, urgent tone, "that's the third time those white women have passed this house in the last hour."

Perry Hamer opened the screen door and stepped into the fragrant yard. Mechanically, he stooped and picked the muddy petunia that had been sent sprawling across the walk by the fury of the storm. His big hand shook the flower gently and his eyes searched for the cars. He saw them in the opening beyond the facing church. They were on the highway now, moving swiftly from the quarter.

It was an old white acquaintance who had brought the news that confirmed her fears. "Fannie Lou, the town is getting upset. There's going to be real trouble if those girls aren't careful." She had known it. There was nothing that might change in Ruleville which could escape her. She knew Ruleville like she knew Virgie and Perry, and she could feel danger in her bones. She had watched the cars circling through the quarter, and she had been cautious. When the cars started to be driven by white women, she had become alarmed. Fannie Lou's worry had begun at Oxford when she had met the scrubbed girls. "Oh, Lord, how young," she had thought. But it was when she brought them into the Delta that the worry became irritation, and the irritation anger. She had exploded to McLaurin after three days.

"You know what that means! If those white women say 'go' to their men, their men are gonna 'go'! Those cars out there cruisin' up and down, lookin' so hard, is full of women!"

She limped across the room and slapped the kitchen table sharply. "McLaurin, I spent a whole week with those girls in Ohio. I told them frankly what they had to expect. That just bein' in the Delta was goin' to be a red flag to the whites, let alone livin' here in the quarter. 'When you ain't workin',' I'd say, 'stay inside. Don't go wanderin' into town. It's askin' for trouble!' I told 'em and told 'em. 'It ain't gonna be like home.' They're good kids, and they seemed to understand. But they get down here and nobody's settin' their house on fire, so they act like they're visitin' their boyfriends on college week end!"

She leaned her weight on the table and glowered at the night through the window. Her voice was throaty and low. "You know what can happen. If some whites laid hands on one of those young girls, every Negro man in Ruleville would be in trouble. That kind of trouble kills people in Mississippi. And what would become of the Movement then?"

She shook her head in exasperation. "It's just as if I never said nothin' to them at Oxford! They sit out under the trees in the back yard playin' cards with the Negro boys. Why, that back yard *faces* the hospital! Or they stand around in the front in groups, chattin' and laughin'! Some of them even wave at cars as they drive by! They cut through white property to get to town. And they go to town to buy curlers and cokes!"

McLaurin nodded. "The real trouble is that we still got a lot of extra folks here. In another day or so they'll be moving over to Shaw, and the Freedom School classes will start here. But I'll talk to them in the morning."

She sank heavily onto the chair at the end of the table. "Mac, I'll tell you the truth! I'm worried sick. You got to spell out the rules for them. All of this just ain't real for them yet. Then, if they can't obey the rules, call their mothers and tell them to send down their sons instead!"

Perry Hamer had opened his home to us from the first day. Quietly, he and Virgie had stepped aside as Dale had set up communications in the parlor. The Hamer home had become the nerve center of all our activity, and in those first days there was a constant flurry of ringing phones and clattering typewriters. The kitchen was a hive of odd-hour eating, and the porch was the hangout for passing newspaper correspondents and students. At almost any hour, a cluster of volunteers and townspeople from the quarter were sprawled in the saving shade of the pecan tree. For Mr. Hamer, the transformation of his home and the destruction of his privacy were but two more phenomena in the disorder of his living. From the day his wife had gone to apply to register, his life had become a crazyquilt of violence, exhilaration, and despair. Her refusal to withdraw her name from the registrar's rolls had torn the even fabric of their life to pieces. Her boss had spelled it out, plain. "I'm not gonna have you registerin' to vote, Fannie Lou! You go down tomorra and tell 'em to take your name off that list!" And she had answered with a passion that had surprised them both. "But you don't understand. I'm not registerin' for *you*. I'm registerin' for *me*!"

After seventeen years as timekeeper on the plantation, she had been fired. Two weeks later, Perry's thirty years at the plantation cotton gin were over as well. He accepted the changes with the quiet, apprising calm that he wore like a protective garment. For a Mississippi Negro, life at best was a mean and burdensome path. If you were a man like Perry Hamer, you walked that path with a gentle stubbornness, knowing that the path usually moved uphill. Few things about "Mr. Charlie's" world deceived him, but his knowledge rested behind his listener's eyes, and he walked his stony path without breaking his stride. No one knew better than he what it was to live the marginal life of the Mississippi Negro. One step from utter poverty, a half-step from the wrath of the white community, he had learned long ago to mask his hurt and to bridle his anger. Now that the job he had held for so long had been snatched from him, he was dependent on occasional part-time work to keep the family together. Like most Negro men in the Delta, he lived with the knowledge that he was incapable of providing properly for his wife and child.

"I drink," he told me one day. He said it simply, without apology. "When I work, I don't drink. But when I'm not working, I like to drink."

A few days after Dale and Dennis had moved into the Hamer home, Mayor Dorrough drove up to the house. Perry rose from the bench under the pecan tree and stood silently. Tall and heavy-set, he was a handsome mahogany figure in his clean overalls. Dorrough's glance flicked past him to the porch where Dennis was typing. His nostrils dilated, and a small vein throbbed between his bushy eyebrows. He continued to watch Dennis, but his words were dripping with contempt and were directed to Perry Hamer.

"How do you feel having white men sleepin' in your house?"

Mr. Hamer remained where he stood. His dark, soft voice sounded clearly through the yard.

"I feel like a man." His eyes were calm and his voice was level. "Because they treat me like a man."

Of more than a hundred drawings that I made that summer, only two contain a fleeting image of Fannie Lou Hamer. One needs at least a few moments of repose to make a portrait sketch, and repose was as foreign to Mrs. Hamer as luxury. The two sketches I did make were done at

Mrs. Fannie Lou Hamer and friends.

eight in the morning, just before her day erupted. Even so, one of them shows her instructing two Ruleville men how to fill out the registration form they would be given in Indianola!

All my memories of Fannie Lou Hamer are ones filled with frenetic movement and gigantic energy. The kinetic quality that surrounded the woman moved out in waves, setting in motion all who were in their path. Watching Mrs. Hamer was not spectator sport. In a flash you were caught up, enlisted, and going somewhere important. Fast!

I had first heard of her from McLaurin. "She's only been in the Movement about two years. But she's something! If she's not here aggravating Mayor Dorrough or running for Congress, she's raising money in Detroit, speaking in New York, or testifying in Washington!" He smiled, nodding his head. "Man, I managed her campaign when she ran for Congress against Jamie Whitten. We got all over this district. And there were lots of days that we shared a bottle of pop for dinner because we needed money for gasoline." He grinned. "Just wait till you hear her sing 'Go Tell It On the Mountain'! You can hear her sing in Williams Chapel if you're standin' in front of Eastland's bank in Ruleville!"

From the moment she arrived from Oxford, mothering her brood of teachers for the Freedom School, black and white Ruleville knew that Fannie Lou was back. Her compact, heavy body was immediately recognized, and her booming voice, scolding, singing, or laughing, was freedom itself. Her sufferings and unbowed spirit had made her a legend in the Movement. Like her voice, her spirit was bigger than life. I recall the morning at the Freedom School, when I had settled against a tree to start a drawing. Fred Miller was just beginning a discussion of nutrition with the assembled ladies when Mrs. Hamer came roaring up to the group like a locomotive, shedding steam, water, and noise. Fred paused in mid-sentence, pop-eyed, as she bore down on the class. In a moment she stood panting beside him, her large bosom rising and falling with excitement.

"I'm sorry, Fred," she bellowed, "I don't like to interrupt your class. But since seven this mornin' my house and yard has been full of women waitin' for the food and clothes that's been sent from the North. And a pack of them women never even been once to Indianola to try and register to help themselves!" She wiped the sweat that cascaded down her face with a large handkerchief, and caught her breath. Her deep voice had a surging cadence that moved effortlessly from conversation to public utterance. "Now, I know that you ladies that's here in the Freedom School understand how important it is for us to keep poundin' on that registrar's door. It's even more important than class. Some of you, though, hasn't been down for a long time. Like you, Mrs. McDonald. And you, Mrs. Davis." Her yellow eyes raced around the group, her timekeeper memory recalling exactly who, when, and how often. "I loaded three cars at my house already, and they're on their way to the courthouse. I told those ladies that no food and no clothes was goin' to be distributed till all the cars come back from Indianola." Somehow, the group was being propelled toward the side of the road. Mrs. Hamer's voice sang out. "Now, we got Len's car and Tracy's. Which ones is goin' with Tracy?" The thought of the waiting cartons combined with a reluctance to tangle with this fierce partisan, and in moments my car was filled.

By two-fifteen we were back in Ruleville, and the thirty women were being warmly welcomed by Fannie Lou Hamer. She stood on the step to her porch and shouted loudly above the milling women in her yard.

"These thirty women know that the way we're goin' to change things here in the Delta, here in Mississippi, is by getting' the vote. Folks up North want to help us free ourselves, and that's why they send these boxes. Anybody who loses his job because he tries to register to vote is goin' to be helped. Anybody who tries to help by standin' up—goin' to Indianola—is goin' to be helped." Her face scanned the crowd, and she

Fred Miller leading a discussion about nutrition at the Freedom School

pointed at the cars, parked at the edge of the lawn. "Who's gonna go with us tomorra when we drive down to the county seat?"

On a furiously hot Sunday morning I drove to Mrs. Hamer's home. I had offered to escort her to church, and she was dressed and waiting. She was encased in a silk print, and her ample body strained at the shiny fabric. She was powdered and brushed, and had even struggled into a pair of leather pumps. In vain she fanned herself as she sat on the edge of her bed, but there was no relief from the furnace of the July morning. She grinned as she saw me enter the room. "Good morning, Tracy! I'm ready!"

I took her arm, and we made our way across the yard to the car. She favored one leg, and I asked whether it was an injury that remained from the police beating she had received some months before.

"Oh, no," she smiled. "This is from a polio attack I had when I was a child."

I climbed into the car and turned on the air conditioning. She sighed and closed her eyes, smiling.

"Where do you want to go to church, Mrs. Hamer? I promise to drive slow!"

She opened her eyes and grinned. "Well, there's a little country church 'bout halfway between here and Drew that I've been meanin' to visit. A nice little minister who I'd like to talk with. Is that too far?"

I laughed at the calculation in her eye. "No, ma'am, it's not too far."

We drove slowly through the quarter, waving at the starched families who were strung out along the roads on the way to church, and turned north on the highway toward Drew. Three miles up the road we turned onto a small dirt road that wound through cotton fields. Standing in the shade of a grove of cottonwoods was the tiny rural church. Four old and dusty cars were parked in the road as I wheeled my Chevvy into the shade. Through the open windows we could hear the young minister's high-pitched reading and the sonorous murmur of the congregation's response.

Mrs. Hamer's hoarse "Good mornin'!" to the men at the entrance echoed through the tiny building. Fannie Lou Hamer was a celebrity in the Delta, and I was probably the first white man ever to attend a service in the church. Our entry was about as unobtrusive as a platoon of tanks.

One look at Fannie Lou's purposeful mien must have convinced the young country pastor that he was in for a trying morning. He paused, smiled tentatively, and then plunged ahead in his reading from Exodus. "And I will dwell among the children of Israel, and will be their God. And they shall know that I am the Lord their God that brought them forth out of the land of Egypt, that I may dwell among them: I am the Lord their God."

His voice dropped, and he closed the book. "This ends our readin' from Chapter Twenty-nine." His eyes lifted and he smiled at us. "I'm right pleased that Mrs. Fannie Lou Hamer has joined our service this mownin'. We are all happy to see you, Mrs. Hamer, and your friend. Would you like to say a few words to the congregation?"

Mrs. Hamer rose majestically to her feet. Her magnificent voice rolled through the chapel as she enlisted the Biblical ranks of martyrs and heroes to summon these folk to the Freedom banner. Her mounting, rolling battery of quotations and allusions from the Old and New Testaments stunned the audience with its thunder. "Pharoah was in Sunflower County! Israel's children were building bricks without straw—at three dollars a day!" Her voice broke, and tears stood in her eyes. "They're tired! And they're tired of being tired!"

Suddenly the rhetoric ceased, and a silence rushed into the room. Her finger trembled as she pointed to the shaken minister, and every eye fastened on the man in the pulpit. Fannie Lou's voice was commanding, but its passion came pure from her committed heart. "And you, Reverend Tyler, must be Moses! Leadin' your flock out of the chains and fetters of Egypt—takin' them *yourself* to register—*tomorra*—in Indianola!"

16

Late one afternoon I sat rocking in the Williams' doorway. Sharon crawled about the parlor, shoving shiny pot covers across the worn, brown linoleum. The carillon in the Baptist Church across town was sounding for Vespers, and the old, beautiful hymns winged through the weary quarter. I wondered if the Baptists knew or cared that the Negroes who couldn't enter their church doors were enjoying their music.

A loud peal of laughter and a raised scornful voice broke my golden reverie. Sharon scrambled across the room and leaned against the locked screen door, peering to see her grandma. Mrs. Williams came trudging down the street, carrying on spirited conversations with the neighbors who sat on their porches or stoops.

"Oh, yes, ma'am! I just did see it on the television! Glory be!"

Her great laugh rang up and down the street.

"Oh, my, yes! All of them senators gathered 'round! And repasentatives! An' then Presiden' Johnson signed the bill!"

She was at the step now, and her voice was etched with acid. "*Now* some scaird folks can stop bein' scaird, and stand up! It's the *law*! Presiden' Johnson has signed the Civil Rights Bill!"

The day following the signing was a big day for Ruleville. At least it was a big day for that churning, black community that makes its way unseen through the days of white Ruleville. "Huck Finn" and four Congressmen came to town. And for a while not even Mayor Dorrough knew they were there.

"Huck" arrived about two-fifteen in the afternoon when he joined the first literature class at the Freedom School. He was introduced to two sixteen-year-old girls, a nineteen-year-old boy, and a lady of twenty-seven. A bright-eyed sparrow of a woman, Liz Fusco, was the hostess who made everybody comfortable. With charm and humor, she read aloud from the Twain volume. To her wondering class, "Huck," "Tom," and "Nigger Jim," were presented as old and warm friends.

The Freedom School had gotten started that morning at eight-fifteen. Seven elderly women eagerly responded as Linda Davis began the exciting journey that would teach them to read. "These are sounds," she said. "I'll say them, then you say them. We'll go slowly. There's no hurry. Now. Ah! Ah! Ah! Ah!"

The women peered through their glasses or squinted as the sunlight touched the sheet that Linda held in front of them. They cleared their throats and very softly repeated back: "Ah. Ah. Ah. Ah."

"You're doing fine," said Linda. "Ay! Ay! Ay! Ay!"

"Ay! Ay! Ay! Ay! Ah! Ah! Ah! Ah!" Literacy class in Ruleville.

Absorbed now, they answered back. "Ay! Ay! Ay! Ay!"

In the next room, a dozen four-through-seven-year-olds were discovering the delights of the new shelves. Heidi Dole, her smiling pretty face animated with pleasure, was handing books to the bright-eyed youngsters. They would curl up on the floor and excitedly thumb through the volumes in search of pictures and color. A world beyond the Delta began to unfold, and a wonderful silence fell in the room. Heidi's gentle voice said, "These books are yours. We can find all sorts of things in them. You can always come and use them here. And, if we take care of them, you can even take some of them home to read. In your own homes." She tucked her feet under her and picked up a book. "Why don't you all gather around, and we'll read this one together."

Australian Kirsty Powell with two students.

At two in the afternoon the session for the school-age children began. In groups of three and four, teachers led their students to areas of the lawn where they might discuss and question without interrupting the progress of another group. Books, pencils, papers—the paraphernalia of learning—sprinkled the hard-packed yard with a confusion of color. The excited talk of the enthusiastic teachers mingled with the suppressed excitement of the Negro children. One watched the young teachers, bending to the task, starting to probe, to move, to make curious. The youngest children were quickest to be fired. Their surprised laughter and exclamations showed contact was being made. The older boys and girls shyly smiled, seriously frowned, or dropped their eyes. No white teacher had ever taught them, and the northern speech sounded hard and strange in their ears. And no teacher had ever reached out toward them with such ardor and trust. It was new, but not uncomfortable. They watched from lowered lids, said little, and noticed everything.

I laughed as I moved through the clusters of kids. America's most verbal students were teaching her least verbal children, and words that had been useful on campus were suddenly embarrassing and pompous. I shuddered as I heard words like "dichotomy" and "incongruous," but as I watched I realized that most of what they were saying was striking sparks. Even during that first afternoon one could hear the vocabularies becoming simpler as the young teachers found common ground with their younger students. At last the self-doubting that had badgered so many of the teachers since Oxford was being removed in the actual

Lucia Guest from North Carolina leads a typing class in the Delta.

*Books for the
Freedom Schools in
Sunflower County.*

confrontation with their students. Finally, they were beginning to do what they had come so far to do.

The Congressmen arrived later. Len Edwards' father, Congressman from the Ninth Congressional District in California, drove in by himself. Having called from Memphis, news of his coming had leaked via the telephone central to the office of Mayor Dorrough. His Honor had immediately placed calls to Len, who failed to answer the suddenly interested Mayor's requests for information. "Why should I answer his call?" asked Len indignantly. "Last week he was saying we set Williams Chapel on fire!"

It was a long and frustrating day for the Mayor. Not receiving hard information as to when the Congressman was to arrive in his little town, he stationed himself at the entrance to the quarter. He had sat for hours and failed to recognize Mr. Edwards when he moved into the quarter in a rented car. Worse still was the arrival of three more Congressmen early that evening, sweeping up to Williams Chapel behind the flashing red lights of the county sheriff's escort!

All four Congressmen, Ryan of New York, Hawkins, Burton, and Edwards of California, had been enthusiastic partisans of the Civil Rights Bill that had been passed the previous day, and they were touring Mississippi to show visible support for the workers who were trying to make civil rights universal. It was a remarkable evening of emotion and dedication. For the men from Washington, here in this steaming chapel in the Delta, was made manifest what had seemed so abstract only hours before. They spoke but briefly, for they were moved beyond words by the naked love and trust that surged from the audience. In that strange summer the Mississippi Negro was finally finding allies. Not one of the five Mississippi Congressmen had ever come to address the Negroes in Ruleville. But there, in Williams Chapel, were four Congressmen from New York and

California! I watched the hands reach out as the heartbreaking "We Shall Overcome" soared from the tiny, scarred church. I wondered if the white folks across the highway, tucked behind their spacious lawns, walking the broad, shaded avenues, got the news: "Huck Finn and Four Congressmen Visited Ruleville Today." I wondered if Mayor Dorrough would tell them.

17

At three in the afternoon, on July 14, Jim Dann was picked up by the Drew Police Chief. He was told that he was breaking a city ordinance by distributing leaflets. The leaflets announced the first mass meeting to be held in Drew. It was scheduled for two hours later. A short, stocky, prematurely balding youngster, Dann fought to control his temper. The sight of the officious chef enraged him. His contempt for Mississippi police was matched only by his inability to disguise it. With a tight and controlled voice he answered, indignation edging each word.

"There is no city ordinance that prevents me from handing out leaflets to people on their property. That's what I was doing."

The chief pursued his lips, pondering the technicalities. He stood up abruptly. "Let's go. The Mayor wants to see you."

Dann grinned as he related the story to me later that afternoon. "I wasn't really arrested," he said. "Just 'picked up.' They were trying to frighten us off. The ordinance is just one more way they can keep literature they don't approve of from reaching the public."

"Did the Mayor give you a hard time, Jim?"

He leaned against a warped support of the Freedom School porch and cocked his head. "Well, let's see. He said that 'livin' with niggers was un-American and anti-Christian,' and that anyone who did 'was a Communist and a disgrace to the white race.'"

I knew that Dann had temporarily interrupted his studies for a Ph.D. in history to work in Mississippi.

He shook his head and laughed. "What really bugged the Mayor was my answer to the 'great question.' He actually asked it! 'Would you want your sister marryin' a nigger?' When I told him I wouldn't mind, I thought he'd have a stroke!"

They had released him with a warning, and he was with us when we returned for the meeting at five in the afternoon.

McLaurin had not yet been able to wheedle the use of a church in Drew, so he had called the meeting for the churchyard. We parked our cars on the side road and approached the church grounds on foot. The leaflets announcing the meeting had raced through the Negro sections, and now people lined the street. Teen-agers had gathered in the church-yard, waiting, but the men of the quarter stood silently across the road in front of the poor bars and cafés. In the middle of the street I saw the police chief's car, and the police pick-up truck. Two additional policemen on foot stood facing the yard. An ominous hushed watchfulness held the block. McLaurin moved as though there were no one there but us. As the students grouped around him in the yard, he started a spirited clapping. His voice slapped at the silence of the street.

> *We are soldiers in the army,*
> *We've got to fight although we have to cry.*

The teen-agers and the students joined in the singing, and the rhythm reached out among the waters.

> *We've got to hold up the freedom banner,*
> *We got to hold it up until we die.*

The song surged, building: "We are soldiers—of the army—we've got to fight—"

A few women, one carrying a baby, joined the singers. Kids who had raced from my camera only ten days before were jiggling and clapping around the students. They giggled as they noted the flushed faces of the police, and they watched McLaurin with wide and wondering eyes.

The song changed, and the voices were louder now, more insistent. The sound, swelled by the increasing numbers, was braver. It beat against the rows of silent men.

This little light of mine,
I'm gonna let it shine!

McLaurin began to speak as the clapping ceased. He addressed the churchyard, but his words were winged across the street. "We're havin' a peaceful meetin'—on church property—and the police there are tryin' to harass us. What are they afraid of?"

The police chief stepped from his car, and the patrolmen on foot moved beside him. They stood silent, arms folded, twenty feet from McLaurin. McLaurin moved through the crowd on the lawn and stopped at the edge of the sidewalk. His words were boldly directed at the men standing on the other side, and he ignored the phalanx of the law that stood between. "What they're afraid of is that you're gonna rise! That you're gonna say, 'I'm a man! Treat me like a man!' Now, we're havin a meetin', and they're afraid you're gonna cross that road and join us. Like men! That you're gonna act like men, not boys! And they're afraid of that! Are you gonna let them see that you're afraid? That you won't join these kids and women?"

The chief stood impassive, his eyes glued on the young Negro whose voice was lashing the men. The police about him shuffled nervously, their armpits were damp stains on their shirts, and their lips were dry. But no one moved across the road.

McLaurin abruptly turned his back, and started a clapping chant.

Which side are you on, boys?
Which side are you on?

Three of the Negro girls from Ruleville who had come to work with us in Drew picked up the verse. They seemed to hurl it at the men who still stood silent.

Oh people can you stand it,
Tell me how you can.

Will you be an Uncle Tom
Or will you be a man?

The crescendo of sound infected the kids up and down the block, and more kept spilling into the yard. Mike Yarrow and Fred Miller moved through the youngsters, handing out song sheets. The surging excited crowd had moved on to the sidewalk when the chief pushed his way into the chanting kids and grabbed Yarrow and Miller. "You're under arrest for handin' out leaflets on a public street without a license." He pushed the boys toward the pick-up truck as the tension and the noise riffled the crowd. The chant rose louder:

Don't "Tom" for Mister Charlie,
Don't listen to his lies

'Cause black folks haven't got a chance
Until they organize!

Now the chief and the two police moved swiftly back into the singing, swaying youngsters. Gretchen, Charley Scattergood, Landy McNair, and Jim Dann were hustled toward the pick-up, arrested for "blocking the sidewalk." The song ended on a ragged note. The excited chatter stilled. John Harris was being led toward the truck by a policeman. The young Negro student paused as he moved to climb into the cab of the truck. He turned an angry face at the Negro men who still stood rooted.

"If you register and vote, you won't have to elect stupid public servants like this one!" He climbed in beside the furious policeman as Gretchen and Charley began to clap and sing in the back. The crowd picked up the beat and the song followed the truck down the dusty road.

Ain't gonna let no po-lice
turn me round,
turn me round,
turn me round—

McLaurin had removed his sunglasses. He stood on the edge of the grass and he spoke to the men who faced him. His eyes were wide and young, more vulnerable than I would have imagined. His voice was imploring, urgent. "We want all the responsibilities of citizenship. Not tomorra! Now! Not next year. Now! You're payin' first-class taxes, but you're lettin' Mister Charlie keep you second-class citizens! If you stay there—if you don't sign up to go down to register to vote in Indianola—you say to the white man, 'Don't treat me like a man. Treat me like a boy!'" His voice was hoarse, and the tears shone in his wide eyes. "We've got to stand up."

He moved past the motionless police and into the crowd of sullen men. From one to another he moved, a stubborn gadfly, shaming, cajoling, holding out the Freedom Registration form that no one would sign. I ached for McLaurin. And I wept for the silent men.

Gretchen was to be separated from the men and sent to the jail in Indianola. It seemed a needless risk to have her jailed alone, so we raised the bond among us and bailed her out. To her this was male chauvinism, and she was furious with all of us.

I was worried when the angry police had driven John to jail. "Accidents" happen often in Mississippi, particularly to Negroes who speak out. But he had merely been penned with the rest of the students in the single concrete cell that was the Drew jail.

John had taken charge. As second in command to McLaurin he assumed responsibility for the group.

"We're going to be arraigned at nine in the morning according to that cop outside. When they ask how you plead, you say 'not guilty.' And you sign no statement till you've been allowed to see your lawyer." He paused, and glanced at the sweaty kids crouched around him. "Just hope the lawyer gets here before the hearing."

The excitement of the afternoon fled with the last light. Darkness closed on the tiny blockhouse, bringing with it the first apprehension. They could watch the cars move slowly past the little stockade. Word had flown through Drew that seven of the "mixers" were over in the jail. Only a tall wire fence, topped with some strands of barbed wire, separated them from the road. John Harris measured the distance. No more than twenty feet, he fretted. An easy lob if someone wanted to throw anything from a passing car.

It was a long, uncomfortable night. Sleep was fitful, and they thrashed awkwardly in the cell, trying to get rest. By first light, they were achy with fatigue and hungry. The exhilaration that had sustained them was chilled in the early morning damp. John stared at the pale salmon sky that was framed in the barred window. He remembered McLaurin pleading with the men to cross. McLaurin's voice filled his ears. "You say to the white man, 'Don't treat me like a man. Treat me like a boy.'" Those poor bastards, he thought. Those poor, poor bastards.

By eight they had been moved to the police station. As they filed in, John sought in vain for someone who might be a COFO lawyer. His face brightened as he saw Gretchen and me hurrying across the road toward the station. The chief, looking choleric and angry, was about to start the proceedings. Harris caught my eye. Soundlessly, he mouthed the words: "Where's the lawyer?" I shook my head and opened my hands. We had phoned Jackson and they had promised that someone would be there. I glanced at the wall clock. It was nine o'clock.

The chief stared distastefully at the camera that hung from my neck. "Nobody allowed in here except the prisoners," he said shortly.

I stepped to the door and almost collided with the two breathless lawyers as they bolted into the station. I grinned at the students and stepped outside into the heat of the morning.

The tire was flat when I reached the car. The morning heat had increased, stoked by a glowering yellow disk that made you squint behind your sunglasses. The scattering of whites who had lingered on the sidewalk, peering into the dirty windows of the station house during the arraignment, lounged under the canopy and watched. I was soaked and filthy by the time I threw the torn tire into the trunk. The door of the station swung open, and the police chief led the boys toward the two cars parked next to mine. I reached quickly for the Leica that lay on the front seat and stepped into the road as the chief approached. He stopped short, and the boys halted abruptly behind him. His face was red and angry, and he poked a stubby finger in my direction.

"Don't you take one damn picture if you don't want to lose that camera!"

I lowered the camera and stepped aside. He moved angrily across the hot pavement. Jim Dann winked as he opened the door of the police car and climbed in. I watched closely. The boys all appeared disheveled, but only John Harris looked haggard and upset. The two cars pulled out, moved down the shaded avenue, turning left finally to meet the highway which ran south toward Indianola. The men in front of the station had stepped to the curb as the police cars turned from sight. My Chevvy stood alone on the block, and I glanced quickly up and down the street. Nothing moved, and I felt dizzy with the glare. As I slammed the trunk I noticed a scrawl on the dusty metal. "FREEDOM NOW!" There was no time to wipe it away, for the men at the curb were starting across the pavement. I started the car and pulled out fast. "FREEDOM NOW!" Jesus! It must have been one of the kids at the Freedom School.

The men stood watching me as I moved into the tunnel of shade, their faces masked by the shadow of their wide straw hats. "FREEDOM NOW!" I let out a deep breath. Go live with teen-agers!

I pulled to a stop at Seal's Grocery. The bell tinkled as I pushed into the tiny store. Seal's daughter grinned as I entered. She was a merry fifteen-year-old, and her eyes were bright and alive. I noticed a "One Man— One Vote" button pinned to her blouse. She caught my glance.

"I got it at the mass meeting last night," she said very quietly.

Mr. Seal moved from behind the counter, all business.

"Yes, sir, what can I do for you?"

His daughter moved abruptly to the front of the store and I noted the cool, veiled look behind Seal's wire-rimmed glasses.

"I've got some nice, fresh country sausage this morning," he said.

"No, thanks. Just a cold, cold Coke! I think I'm dying!"

The barest smile touched his lips as he watched me fish a wet bottle from the cooler.

"He's a card-carrying member of the NAACP," one of the women at the Freedom School had said. "But he runs that bus to the plantation and makes a heap of money doin' it. Nothin' Mistuh Charlie wants to know he can't find out from Mistuh Seal."

We wanted to patronize Negro businesses while we were in the Delta, but there were so few. And too often we felt that the right people were not running them. I glanced back at the little store as I climbed into the car. Mr. Seal had moved to the front, and I could see his big head shaking vigorously, and his mouth noiselessly opening and closing. His daughter's back was to the plate-glass window. Her head was tilted back, and she stood very still and very straight.

I wheeled under the overhang at the gas station, rolled past the tanks, and stopped in the knife-edge of shade thrown by the building. I moved to the rear of the car and with a paper towel started to wipe away the scrawled "FREEDOM NOW!" Two white women stood watching from the office door. The taller was blonde and pretty. She tossed back her hair saucily and called over to me. "You don't look like the others!"

Her chin was up, and she threw the words like a dare. I finished wiping off the trunk as I watched her. She was young, late twenties, I thought, and she was very pregnant. Her companion seemed taken aback that the blonde had spoken to me. She was tiny and looked embarrassed, and her fingers fussed with her linen purse.

I wiped my hands on the toweling and walked slowly across the soft asphalt. I stopped directly in front of them and said, "Beg your pardon?"

The blonde flushed, but stood her ground.

"I said you don't look like the rest of them!"

I grinned at her. "I'm just like the rest of them. I'm twenty years older than they are, but I'm just like the rest of them!"

She giggled, and the tension seemed to ease from her shoulders. The sunburned skin around her eyes crinkled, and she stole a quick look at her companion. Her face swung back to mine. "Take off your sunglasses," she commanded. "I've got questions to ask you, and I want to see your eyes."

Obediently, I removed the glasses and squinted down at her in the noon glare.

"What would you like to ask me?" I inquired.

"Well, what are you doing here in Ruleville?"

"I'm spending the summer making drawings. I'm covering the kids who came down here to work. I'm an artist."

She cocked her head with interest. "Who are you bein' an artist for?"

"CBS."

Her eyes were steady now, and the playfulness had been turned off. "Would you answer me honest—would you really talk with me?"

A trickle of perspiration moved down the small of my back, and I was aware for the first time in days that I was stained with sweat and dust. There was an agreeable feminine radiance about the woman, and she made you remember that you were a man. I smiled at her and nodded. "Sure. Let's talk. What's bothering you?"

She pouted and tossed her hair back. "We can't talk here!"

I looked about the deserted station elaborately. Teasing, I said, "Why not?"

"Oh, for heaven's sake!" she exploded. "This is a gas station!"

She paused, uncertainly, and then took a breath. She glanced quickly at her companion, and then seemed to make a private decision. Her eyes were challenging as they moved to my face. "Would you come to my house?"

Her friend's eyes widened, but she remained silent.

"Well, now. That's the first invitation I've had from the white community since I arrived!" I said lightly.

She flushed. "Now don't start that!"

"Before I accept your kind invitation, you ought to know that if I come I'm liable to jeopardize your position in the community. When I drive out of the quarter," I said, "I'm often followed."

The blonde shook her head in annoyance. "Don't be silly. Everybody in Ruleville knows me. Just come."

"Thank you. Can I bring some of the kids I'm living with? You'd like them."

"Heavens, no!" Her eyes were so wide with horror that I burst out laughing.

"When would you like me to come?" I asked.

"One-thirty. Emily, you come, too." She smiled at me. "My name is Allison Cutler. What's yours?"

18

Jerry Tecklin stared at me. The notebook lay open on his lap. "The Cutlers are important people. Allison Cutler is married to Billy Cutler, a family that reaches way back in Mississippi. His daddy was a very big wheel in the Delta." He closed the notebook. "You're really going to their home?"

I nodded. Dale picked up the Ruleville phone book and wrote down the address and phone number. "If you're not back by four-thirty, we'll come looking for you."

The Cutlers' house was adjacent to the highway, five minutes north of town. I parked the car at the dead end of the small road and looked about me. It was a new neighborhood, pleasant and unpretentious. The Cutlers' modest house suited the street. As I climbed from the Chevvy, the aluminum screen door swung open, and Allison waved cheerily. "Hi, Tracy! Come on in!"

The living room was cool and inviting. The slipcovers were bright, and the furniture was simple and comfortable. Billy Cutler rose from the corner of the couch and met me in the middle of the room. He was a large, taciturn man, six foot three, perhaps two hundred and twenty pounds. I noted the heavily muscled arms and the belly that was beginning to paunch. He looked like an ex-athlete, probably a tackle or a fullback who had never been really lean. His face was set and his eyes were still.

"Allison told me about you, Tracy. I'm glad to meet you. I'm Billy Cutler, and I'd be obliged if you'd call me Billy."

We shook hands and he nodded to Allison's morning companion. "You've met Em?"

She smiled shyly, her eyes alert. "We met Mr. Sugarman at Sandy's gas station, Billy." Her voice was light and musical. Sandy is my brother, Mr. Sugarman."

A Negro maid brought coffee and noiselessly disappeared back into the kitchen. Allison sat, Buddha-like, on the floor, pouring coffee. Her eyes were bright, and one could see that she was curious and excited. She handed me my coffee.

"I'm glad you came, Tracy."

"I appreciate your inviting me here. It's nice being in a room like this again." I set the saucer carefully on the edge of the coffee table and looked at the Cutlers. "I'd like to talk with you. But I don't think we can talk honestly if I don't level with you to start with."

Billy Cutler sat stirring his cup, and his eyes were careful. I cleared by throat, and started again. "I told you at the gas station that I was covering the summer project for CBS, Allison. That's true. But I don't want to misrepresent myself to any of you. I'm not just a reporter who happened to get assigned to Mississippi."

Billy sipped his coffee, one heavy arm draped across the rear of the couch.

"I'm here because I want to be here. I believe in what these kids are here to do. I told CBS I was coming, and then they said they could show the work. You all deserve to know that. I'm not neutral."

Allison's eyes were level over her coffee cup. She put down the cup and her face was serious. "I told Billy I had invited you home because there were questions to be answered. You're living with these people, Tracy, and we'd still like to get some answers. Billy?"

He hiked himself forward on the couch, and his elbows rested on his knees. His resonant voice rolled quietly across the room. "Ally's right. We would like answers. We suspected you don't share our point of view." He hesitated for a moment, and then plunged ahead. His face darkened, and his voice took on a timbre. "Maybe you can tell us how these kids can presume to come into our state, not knowing our people or our customs, and tell us how to live our lives." His voice was more troubled than angry.

"Well, Billy, I went through the orientation course with them in Ohio, and all I can say is that they're not here to change your way of life. They're here to help the Negro in Mississippi change his way of life. They think they can do it in two ways. The first is by teaching him the responsibilities of citizenship—the importance of voting. The second is by enriching his education so he has some sense of American history, and his own history as well. These kids are here to work in the Negro community, not the white community."

Allison sniffed loudly. "Thank goodness! I never saw such a filthy bunch of people! Where did they find these creeps?"

I looked at her face. Her nose was wrinkled with disgust.

"At Harvard," I said dryly. "And Swarthmore. And Stanford. And Reed. And Howard. Look, Allison, these kids aren't creeps. For the most

White Mississippians, July, 1964

part they're middle-class kids from our best schools. They're the only ones who could steal a summer without working. These 'filthy' kids you're talking about are just like all the kids who have been hanging around our house with my teen-age son for the past four years. This is not the sandal and beard contingent, the 'Beats.' These are idealistic youngsters who want to help right what they think is wrong. You drive in to pick up your maid in the Quarter, and you pass these boys and girls working up and down the unpaved roads. You think 'Jesus, what filthy kids! How scruffy!' Think about it. When it's dry, they're dusty. When it's wet, they're muddy. You don't pave roads in the Negro section of town."

"There's no excuse for being unclean," said Allison. "No excuse for looking crummy."

"I won't offer excuses, but I can give you reasons, Allison. And they have nothing to do with the moral fiber of the kids we're talking about. I wonder if you know that only thirty percent of the Negro houses down here have adequate bathing or toilet facilities. In the house I'm staying in there is one cold water tap and no sink. It's hard in hundred-degree heat to keep clean and shaven with cold water in a tin basin. Most of the kids do their laundry in kettles over fires in the back yard. Allison, we're living the life your Negroes live all the time."

She sat silent, her fingers picking idly at the edge of the rug.

"There's one other reason, Allison. These kids are scared. They wake up scared, they go to church scared, they do their jobs scared, and they go to bed scared. These are kids who never had to worry about pick-up trucks with shotguns and wagons with police dogs."

She lifted her eyes from the rug and picked up her half-empty coffee cup. As she replaced it on the table the maid moved quietly into the room to remove the soiled cups and saucers. Allison pushed her hair back from her ears. Her eyes were kindled.

"I saw Len Edwards on TV the night he arrived in Ruleville. He looked like such a nice, clean-cut kid I wanted to bring him home to meet Billy and see our kids. See how we really live. How we really are." She narrowed her eyes and her voice was cutting. "The very next day I saw him walking down a road in Sanctified Quarter with a nigger girl!"

I watched the maid continue to load the tray with the cups and saucers. The hands moved from table to tray without a missed beat.

"I could have killed him!" Allison's hands clenched, and she beat a fast tattoo on the rug. The maid stepped carefully around her and left the room. Allison's chin came up and a mischievous grin touched her lips. She shook her head. "No. I couldn't have killed him. But I wanted to!"

There was a quality to that afternoon. Perhaps it was the mutual wonder that we all shared, the remarkable happening that had allowed this kind of conversation. Not once in the hours together did rancor or personal hostility sour the talk. The intervening days were to witness pain and change and a steeling of resolve on the part of both the Negro and the white community. In that tragic summer of violence and martyrdom I look back to the shaded living room of the Cutlers' as a tiny island where, for a brief moment, one could seek understanding.

Billy had stormed at the northern press. "They crucify us!" He had pounded his fist into the palm of his other hand. "And they lie. I saw a northern paper that said whites had burned down Williams Chapel!" His eyes had searched my face. "Now, you know that's not so! Hell, if we wanted to burn down that church we would have done a better job than that! The truth of the matter is that our white fire truck got out there in ten minutes and put out the fire. And at two in the morning!"

"I'm not going to defend bad journalism, Billy, whether it's in the North or the South. If you say you saw the story, I accept your word. But over twenty churches *have* been burned to the ground already this summer, Billy. And that's not an invention of the northern press! If you're suggesting that Negroes set fire to Williams Chapel, I'm telling you you're wrong. You don't know me, Billy, and you don't have to believe what I tell you. But I know the Negroes in the quarter don't have the money even to repair the damaged steps or repaint, and I know they're heartsick and frightened by the fire."

Emily had listened attentively, and at this point her thin voice piped across the small room. "Well, the Yankee papers certainly do manage to give Mississippi a black eye every change they get! You'd think we invented violence down here!"

"You're wrong," I retorted. "Mississippi gives Mississippi a black eye. What do you think the *Look* editor is going to write when he was chased last Wednesday night from Ruleville to Greenwood, thirty miles, by a carful of whites at ninety miles an hour? I know this guy. He was scared to death! He doesn't have to invent a story about Mississippi, Emily! All he has to do is tell the truth!"

Allison's lips curled in a tight, private smile. She said softly, "Nobody was going to hurt him."

Billy Cutler warmed to my challenges. His large body was poised on the edge of the couch, and he would reach for arguments and responses. "I wish I was better educated so I could say better what I want to get out!" When he would bait me with the high rate of illegitimacy among the Negroes, I would point out the impossibility of middle-class values among people who were eking out a marginal existence. He would frown, and thrust ahead. "I was too smart to go to college, Tracy, so I can't answer you the way I'd like to!" He clung to the image of the child-like, irresponsible Negro as if it were an act of faith. "I know them. They don't want to learn! We build schools for them and they don't use them!" I pointed out that he could hardly criticize the Delta Negro for caring little about an educational system that spent only seventy dollars a year on his education!

"What if the Negro kid does stay in your inadequate Negro high school, Billy? What if he doesn't drop out? What's he going to do in Ruleville after he graduates?"

Billy hunched his shoulders and shook his head.

"I'll tell you, Billy. But you know. There are two factories in Ruleville, and they don't hire Negroes. So he graduates to chop cotton."

Allison's voice was silken. "I told you that, Billy. I told you!" It was a slap that occurred often during that afternoon.

Billy's face was grave, and his eyes winced in concentration. "What bothers me most is you people trying to register *everyone* to vote! Hell, Tracy, what would happen to this state if we let everyone—anyone— vote?"

"Well, what's happened to your state not letting everyone vote? By almost every measurable standard, Billy, Mississippi is fiftieth of fifty."

"But it's ridiculous to think that every nigger who can make his mark should decide how to run this state," he exploded. "It isn't race, it's education! Why, there are whites on my place that I wouldn't let vote!"

I stared at him. "*You* wouldn't let vote? It's not up to you, Billy, to decide who's qualified to vote. The Constitution sets those qualifications. But in Mississippi qualified Negroes have been deprived of their vote, and unqualified whites have been registered. I know, because I know who I've taken up those steps to try and register. And you know, because you live here."

Allison nodded, her face turned toward her husband. Billy stared back. Finally, he cleared his throat, and his words were low. "I'm not going to pretend that what you're saying isn't so, Tracy. There should be the same standard for everybody. But I know that if they give the vote to unqualified people, there's going to be trouble—real trouble—in the Delta."

"But, Billy. This is 1964. There are Negroes who've gone all over the world in the service and come back to Ruleville! You can't tell them they can't vote! Some white registrar with a grammar school education can't deprive people who are better educated than he is because he doesn't approve of Negroes voting! I've taken Negroes down to Indianola who finished high school, and the Man still won't register them! And what about the older folks, the ones who never had a chance to go? They may not read or write well, but they know what the score is in Ruleville. Can you fail to educate people and then penalize them for being uneducated?"

Cutler's gaze was level and unblinking. "There'll be trouble. Real trouble."

He shook his head in exasperation. "What's so hard to explain to you—to people like you—is how much we care for our niggers. You think we're heartless because we segregate our society. I tell you that the nigger prefers it that way, same as we do. We know each other, know what to expect from each other. It's worked out for a hundred years this way." His voice trailed off. He began speaking again, very quietly, and I strained forward to hear. "I've taken nigger kids out of my field, and driven them to school. Not that I couldn't have used more pickers. But they need school! Who put them in the field, Tracy? Me? Hell, no! *Their* folks. Ally can tell you. The football week end we gave up at Ole Miss so I could stay at the bedside of one of the sick nigger children from the plantation. I drove him to the hospital in Mound Bayou. The kid's mama didn't care, and Christ knows who the kid's pa was." His eyes were bright. His voice lifted. "They're not responsible people, Tracy! They're children themselves. They chuck responsibility every chance they get. But we know that down here. They're goodhearted folks most of 'em, goodhearted as most whites I know. Better than some. I've been raised next to them, and I know them. In a way I love them." The room was silent, and a flush of embarrassment touched the heavy, boyish face. "I don't suppose you can believe that."

Allison and Emily had nodded agreement as Billy had spoken. I knew that he had echoed the great thesis which underpinned the "Southern Way of Life." I nodded as well. "You're wrong, Billy, I do believe you. I think you're a good man—a compassionate man—and I believe you. What I don't believe is that your love has helped them. Or Mississippi."

His eyes were quiet, and he leaned back into the corner of the couch, listening.

"You say you love your Negroes. I say you don't respect them. You don't now, you never did, and as a result they don't respect themselves." I pointed at the comfortable room. "If you couldn't provide for Allison and your kids, if you couldn't earn enough even to feed them twelve months a year, you'd despise yourself. Maybe you'd even drink, like so many of the Negro men do. It makes their inadequacy easier to bear. Did you ever wonder why the Negro woman is the backbone of the family, Billy? Because she can find steady work. If the white southerner respected the Negro, he'd see that he learned skills so he could be a stable member of society. Instead, he thinks he's being noble when he goes down to the jail on Monday morning and bails out his 'boy' so he can get him back to chopping."

The lemon-yellow rectangle had edged across the rug as the afternoon had raced away. Now it had moved up the wall, touching the frames of the two oil portraits of the Cutlers. I thought of the sepia photograph on the Williams' wall. I wondered if these portraits had been painted on a honeymoon trip, maybe in New Orleans.

Allison's voice was little, and the words came hushed. "Where do we start?" Her eyes were troubled. "We've got to start, Tracy. But where?"

I told them about the Negro high school and the overcrowded classrooms and facilities, about the lack of vocational courses. "Why not start there? If you were turning out electricians and carpenters and roofers instead of just cotton choppers, the whole Delta would benefit. These folks could bring their kids up in clean houses and with pride. Those kids are going to be neighbors of your kids, Allison."

She nodded, her face was down. Her voice sounded hesitant and muffled. "You can't know—it's so hard. I can't stand their touching me, shoving against me." Her face came up and her eyes were wet and wild. "What can I do?"

"I can't help you, Allison. The world keeps turning, and I guess we have to turn with it. It's easy to get panicked by change unless we look at it realistically. The kind of social integration that you find so hard to face is not going to happen suddenly. Most Negroes in the Delta can't afford to go to restaurants and motels. Besides, they're much more interested in jobs and education and the vote than they are in integrating country clubs! No. The kind of integration that you're going to have to cope with soon, like it or not, will be when four frightened little colored children come to the Ruleville grammar school. Everybody in Ruleville is going to get all upset. But after all, that's all they are. Four frightened children."

The phone rang twice in the kitchen. The maid came to the door and told Allison that I was wanted on the phone.

George Winter's drawl crackled through the phone. "Hey, man, where are you? We've got to go to Drew!" There was a pause, and the Okie voice continued quietly. "You okay?"

"I'm just fine. See you in ten minutes."

I walked to Billy and extended my hand. "I've got to go."

We shook hands, and they followed me to the door.

"Thanks for your hospitality," I told them. "It was a good afternoon."

19

It was four-forty-five when I parked in front of the Freedom School. The seven arrested students had been released on bail at noon, and were sitting along the edge of the porch talking with the two lawyers. Their interviews were over, and the young attorneys were wearily packing the depositions into their briefcases. I walked with them to their car as they were about to set out for Jackson. "Don't go too far," I teased. "We may

Gretchen Schwarz being interviewed by lawyer after her arrest in Drew.

need you in a little while!"

"Don't call us. We'll call you!" said one, laughing. We shook hands, and they drove from the quarter.

George Winter came out on the porch. "Hate to break up your party," he cracked. "Was she nice?"

We loaded three cars with voter registration people and a half-dozen kids from the youth group. Ellie Siegel and Chris Hexter climbed into the rear seat of the Chevvy. For the first time, Freedom School teachers were going to a voter meeting. They were curious and excited.

Newly deputized whites sealed off both ends of the street that faced the churchyard. They sweated under riot helmets, and carried billy clubs and side arms. They looked worried and tense, and their eyes kept moving to the hundreds of Negroes that lined the street and milled in the churchyard. They made me think of the kids who came green from boot camp during the war. I shuddered at all the lethal equipment that hemmed in the restless block.

The singing started the moment we stepped from the sidewalk.

> *Woke up this morning with my mind*
> *Stayed on free-dom!*

The singing was strident. Nervous.

The chief and the police regulars once again dominated the center of the road. Their eyes riveted on McLaurin as he worked the crowd to shouted response. Voices rang with excitement and enthusiasm. "Oh, yes!"

The mounting din broke suddenly as the chief stepped forward. His drawling voice could be heard easily as he spoke with a slow, deliberate enunciation of each word. They were trespassing, and if they did not wish to be arrested for trespassing, they must leave the church grounds immediately. McLaurin's reply was sharp and immediate.

Chris Hexter, Freedom School teacher.

"We have permission from the deacon of the church to hold an out-door meeting on the church grounds."

The chief shook his head. "That permission has been withdrawn by the deacon."

A growl of resentment sounded in the yard. McLaurin led the angry crowd swiftly into the empty lot that bordered the church yard, and the meeting resumed with a rush of sound. Chanting soared as more young people from the road joined the demonstrators. The chief retreated to his car and used his radio. Five minutes later another police car moved through the cordon of helmeted deputies and parked near the chief. A policeman helped an elderly white woman from the front seat and escorted her to the chief. Together they walked to the edge of the hushed crowd. The woman's face was pale and lined. Her mouth was set in a thin colorless line, and her eyes were alarmed.

"This is the lady that owns the property you're on." The voice of the chief was flat and hard. "She wants you off."

McLaurin's frustration and rage exploded. His hoarse voice slashed at the police. "These police aren't used to having Negroes standin' up like men! They're not used to having Negroes refuse to run when they say run!"

The tense crowd responded at every sentence. They closed tightly about the taut figure of the speaker.

"They don't want anything that's gonna change a system that lets them get rich and lets you work from 'cain't to cain't' for three dollars! They don't want change because when you stand up, you're gonna change the things that keep you second class!"

The police edged closer to the walk. The chief's hand rested on his holster and his voice shook. "I'm telling you all for the —"

But McLaurin's furious voice interrupted. "They don't want us to demonstrate peaceably. The Constitution says we have a right to assemble peaceably. That we have a right to request a redress of grievances. But these police say 'no'! They say 'no!' and we're supposed to stop. They say 'no!' and we're supposed to turn around!" He shoved his way through the churning crowd toward the edge of the lawn. "If they want to force us out of the churchyard, force us out of an empty lot, force us into the street so they can arrest us, then we'll go! We'll go into the street! And we'll fill all the jails!"

"Yes! Yes! Oh, yes!" Clapping and chanting, they surged across the walk and into the street. McLaurin turned for a moment, and signaled John Harris to take over. Harris nodded understanding. Deliberately he stepped back on the lawn to avoid arrest. The police herded the stream of clapping and singing people down the dusty ghetto road toward the jail. The song rocketed around the quarter as they moved on. "Woke up this morning with my mind—stayed on freedom!"

Ellie Siegel, Gretchen, and five of the local girls from Ruleville were arrested and sent into segregated cells in Indianola. Chris Hexter, McLaurin, and fifteen other students, members of the Ruleville youth group, and boys from Drew were sent to the county farm in Moorhead.

Liz Fusco was tired, and her ear ached from the pressure of the telephone receiver. She had been on the phone until late in the night. Now it was eight in the morning, and she wearily started the calling again. "Operator, I want to call New Haven, Connecticut."

One of the Freedom School teachers, Kirsty Powell, paused at the screen door on the way to the assembling classes on the lawn. She watched Liz and spoke only when Liz had paused.

"Lucia and I will cover for Chris and Ellie. Don't worry about their classes."

Liz nodded. Kirsty's sunny face and perky Australian twang always cheered me, and I waved from the shadowed hallway. She stepped quickly inside.

"Good morning!" Her voice dropped as Liz spoke into the phone. "How is Liz making out?"

"It's slow," I answered. "Forty-five hundred dollars bail is a lot of dough."

Kirsty shook her head and moved to the door, frowning.

I watched the slim, erect woman step into the bright light of the yard. A grave fourteen-year-old girl who had been standing alone under a tree fell into step with her, and they crossed the grass to the group at the end of the yard. Kirsty's husband was teaching at the University of Pennsylvania, and at the end of the summer they would return to Australia. She was a gifted and sensitive teacher. Despite her obvious foreign tongue, she had made immediate contact with the Negro children of the Delta.

Liz's voice rose in the empty hallway. "In Drew. Yesterday. That's right. Yesterday afternoon." The voice was intense. Her eyes rested on the bulletin board. A SNCC poster showed a hard-eyed Mississippi national guardsman. The block letters underneath asked: "Is He Protecting You?" She frowned, cradling the phone against her cheek.

"No. He's fine. He's all right. Yes, sir. The lawyer was there at the hearing. Two hundred dollars. Right. To me. Yes, you can wire it. F–U–S–C–O. Right. I'll have him call you immediately. Thank you. Good-by."

She scratched an X next to the name on the paper, and her pencil moved down the page. Her face was pale in the dim hall, and a damp film of perspiration glowed on her forehead. A deep weary exhaling of breath fluttered from the small chest.

"Operator. I want to call Swarthmore, Pennsylvania."

The first time I had seen her was in an orientation session at Oxford. Jim Forman was leading a class in questions and answers about the mores of the people we would soon be living with. Her hand had raised timidly, and Jim had nodded toward her. All eyes in the class had rested on the tiny girl with the long braid down her back.

"What if"—her voice had trembled, and she cleared her throat. "What if we don't usually go to church ourselves. Must we go with the family we stay with?"

Jim had smiled kindly and answered that no one expected them to go to church if they had scruples against doing so. But, he added, it was a very good way to get to know your family.

Liz had colored, looking even younger and more naïve than before. I watched her now. Bone tired, she was doing a tough, thankless job, and doing it efficiently and well. When she finished, she would go back to the lawn and resume her class. I remembered thinking that evening in the class at Oxford, "How can they let a child like that go down into Mississippi?"

Liz had stayed for both weeks of orientation at Oxford, and when next I saw her she was arriving in Ruleville as director of the Freedom School. In the very first days it became clear that the birdlike fragility and delicate frame were deceptive; Liz was an able, tough, and aggressive woman.

In the extraordinary atmosphere of the Freedom School, where the turnover in students was high and the skills of the students impoverished, the successful teachers were like Kirsty and Lucia; they had a flexibility and talent for improvisation that delighted and inspired the children. A rigidity of personality made teaching in the volatile atmosphere of the school terribly difficult for structured people like Liz Fusco. She persevered because she felt so deeply the commitment of the summer. When at the end of the summer she moved into administration of the Freedom Schools throughout the state, I thought she had found a niche where she could best use her skills.

I stood on the porch watching the classes. It was a never-ending thrill for me. The enthusiasm of the old women, the curious, eager children, the quick laughter and thrust of the teachers, all made a comforting pledge for the future. Even on this morning, when I knew that twenty-three of the kids were penned in the filth of the county farm and the county jail, I watched the classes and felt good.

The phone rang inside the house, and Liz called my name. Dennis Flanagan's gentle voice sounded in my ear.

"Since you're not in jail, why don't you come over to Shaw?"

"It's probably the only good reason ever to go to Shaw," I bantered. "What do you want my car for?"

"To drive to Cleveland," he laughed. "We've got a lot of folks to carry to the 'Freedom Day.' I thought since most of your people were in jail, you might like a change of scene."

Dennis was a real favorite of mine. During one of the first evenings in the Delta a small group of white Mississippi college students had come to the Hamers' yard. Their intention was to persuade our workers by argument, not violence, to return North. The forensic skill of volunteers like John Harris of Howard University was imposing, and the ensuring bull session was lively. During one heated exchange Dennis had suddenly blurted out, "Frankly, I don't have the courage to be in Mississippi!" From that moment on I had been his fan. I checked out with Liz Fusco and drove the fifteen miles to Shaw.

It was my first look. The rotten shacks made most of the homes in Negro Ruleville seem substantial in comparison. That kind of poverty should have smothered the community in hopelessness. But I knew from Dennis that even in the terrible wasteland of Shaw the Movement had taken root almost immediately upon the arrival of the workers from Ruleville.

The muddy yard in front of the Freedom House was full of middle-aged and elderly ladies in their best clothes. It was noisy and cheerful, and

Pickets.

students moved among them, selecting groups for the waiting cars. Dennis welcomed me in the tiny room he used for communications. "Thanks for coming! We've got a lot more people than wheels!" His voice dropped, and he pushed his dark hair back from his forehead. "Cleveland, Mississippi— in fact all of Bolivar County—has never seen a 'Freedom Day.' We don't know what we'll find when we get there. But they know we're coming."

Our cars left the main highway as we entered Cleveland. Driving slowly and carefully, we worked our way through the Negro section of town. I noticed the venetian blinds in Amzie Moore's house were drawn tight. Nothing inside could be seen from the street. The house wore a veiled look, even in the daylight. My car radio was tuned to the Greenwood, Mississippi, radio station. The announcer was doing a remote broadcast from the scene of the "Freedom Day" in Greenwood. His words crackled, and the noise of shouting could be heard in the background.

The long, steaming, patient wait in Cleveland, Mississippi.

The voice was vibrant and excited and he breathed heavily into the microphone. Angry civil rights workers had apparently defied a local ban on picketing, and the police had moved in force to break up the demonstration. Over a hundred workers were being forced with billy clubs and cattle prods into vans and buses. They were singing and clapping, and the noise rang behind the tense voice of the Greenwood reporter. I snapped off the radio as we moved into the pleasant residential streets that flanked the courthouse, and I glanced at the ladies squeezed into the back seat. If the news from Greenwood had frightened them, they refused to show it. Their faces were calm. Their hands moved only to smooth a skirt or check a strand of hair. Only the young, pregnant woman sitting in the front seat showed her nervousness. She licked her lips and kept shifting her position. Her opaque eyes flicked from one side of the road to the other. "Boy, oh, boy," she breathed heavily. "Boy, oh, boy."

The courthouse was large and imposing, set in a park of old oak trees. The spacious, shaded lawn stretched comfortably from the tan brick building to four streets. Rising in slender elegance on the lawn was a tall, granite pedestal. On its facing were reverential words of memoriam to the Confederate dead, and at its crown stood a lithe Confederate soldier. The whole aspect of the setting was one of dignity and repose. The walks that edged the streets about the courthouse were being patrolled by white-helmeted police auxiliaries. Marching in twos with rifles on their shoulders, their khaki shirts black with sweat, the pleasant park looked as though it was under siege. Police and official-looking civilians moved up and down the walks that laced the green and tramped across the turf. Officers growled into field telephones as overheated auxiliaries stacked rifles. "My God," I said, laughing, "what do they think you ladies are planning to do?"

I wheeled into the arc of the driveway and was immediately challenged by a wide-eyed youngster who stood with a rifle at port arms. Sweat

"Are we free?"
"No!"
"Free-dom!"
"Now!"

ran down his nose, and the heavy helmet kept sliding low over his eyes. He came to my side of the car. "Nobody allowed on the grounds today," he said hesitantly.

I pointed to the crowd of whites who were standing on the far side of the road. "That means them. These folks are just going to the courthouse to register to vote, son." I raced the motor and he stepped back, perplexed. I drove quickly to the entrance, followed by the rest of the cars bearing the ladies from Shaw.

Jonathan Black, a Harvard student from New York, ran the demonstration effectively. His gaunt frame in the blue work shirt and jeans moved restlessly between the back and the side of the courthouse. The eyes behind the black-rimmed glasses were watchful and concerned, and he was keenly sensitive to the tension building in the crowd of whites. The crowd had grown all morning. Now, at noon, they overflowed the opposite walk and edged the pavement as well. The patrolling police marched in twos up and down the walks, and no one crossed over.

In the rear of the courthouse, under a huge oak that blanketed the lawn with shadow, sat the forty applicants from Shaw. One of the students ladled water from a milk can, and several of the girls distributed the sandwiches they had prepared the night before. For the long, steaming day the women sat patiently waiting their turn. Two by two they were admitted by the armed auxiliaries, moving silently up the worn wooden steps of the courthouse to the registrar's office.

At the side entrance of the building, space had been allowed for peaceful picketing. The students, carrying signs demanding justice and the vote, marched in a long, shallow oval. Morris Rubin, a heavy-chested, swarthy student, was the leader of the pickets. As he moved in the sweltering heat, he would raise his head and bellow: "*FREE*-DOM!"

The pickets would respond: *"NOW!"*

Again, the ringing *"FREE-DOM!"*

Once more, the response *"NOW!"*

"IS THIS THE U.S.A.?"

"YES!"

"IS THIS MISSISSIPPI?"

"YES!"

"ARE WE FREE?"

"NO!"

"FREE———DOM!"

"NOW!"

"JIM CROW—"

"MUST GO!"

"JIM CROW——"

"MUST GO!"

"FREE————DOM!"

"NOW!!!"

Moving about the lawn as the afternoon wore on, I was introduced by a reporter to the county attorney, Mr. Valentine. I was struck at once by his good manners in the face of a situation that was difficult and delicate. His uneasy glance would swing from the circling, chanting students to the staring watchers beyond the road. An endless line of cars edged, bumper to bumper, down the wide avenue. The attorney's face was pale in the speckled shade of the oaks. He nodded at the line of cars. His voice was tired and dry. "Folks down here aren't used to seeing picket signs. Even union signs in front of stores." His eyes followed the pickets. Boys and girls, Negroes and whites, they plodded in the afternoon sun. They were singing now, and the song carried across the broad lawns to the stifling streets.

No more Jim Crow——
No more Jim Crow——
No more Jim Crow over me——

He ran a finger under his damp collar and loosened the knot of his tie a little. "It's not like it is up East. We're not used to it." He wiped his sunglasses with an immaculate handkerchief. "I'll tell you the truth, Mr. Sugarman. It's hard to take."

As the clock edged toward four, Valentine came across the grass once more and stood with me near the steps to the courthouse. Like Jonathan Black, he looked spent and tense, and he longed for the day to end soon. "How much longer are they going to demonstrate?" he asked wearily.

"They've got to return these folks to Shaw in shifts," I explained. "They don't have enough cars. Otherwise, they'd be all through. They'll just picket until they're all returned."

He rubbed his chin, and for the first time he smiled. "I'll be glad to let them use my car! It's been a long day."

He was an intelligent and attractive man. It was his fortune to be Bolivar County Attorney when the status quo was being challenged. His whole demeanor indicated that he understood the inevitability of change. But it hurt him. As we chatted, he frowned, seeking honest answers to my questions. "Education. It's going to take education. Not just for the Negroes. No one in Mississippi gets well educated. Black or white."

His eyes followed the students once more, and the soft Mississippi voice was low. "Ordinarily, we're hospitable people. And it makes us feel bad not to welcome strangers in our town to our homes. Some of these young people look real clean-cut. It's a shame that they won't have the chance to meet some of the white folks here in Cleveland." He held out his hand. "I practice law with my dad in that low building across the street there. Next time you're in town," he paused and grinned, "without your friends, come by and see us!"

Unlike Greenwood, Cleveland had behaved well during its "Freedom Day." It had watched the students arrive with the Negroes from Shaw, demonstrate, and depart. Like it or not (and it certainly did not), a civil rights demonstration had been held in Bolivar County.

Mike Yarrow, Swarthmore, Pennsylvania.

At eight the following morning, the Western Union key started to clatter in the back of the Rexall Drug Store. The money orders from California, Illinois, Washington, and Connecticut were arriving in Ruleville. A sulky-faced white boy wrote out the checks and petulantly called out the names.

"Heidi Dole."

"Len Edwards."

The staccato gossip of the key continued.

"Linda Davis."

By eight-thirty the total had reached forty-five hundred dollars, and the clerk was pale and angry. He stared stolidly at the students, refusing even to acknowledge their "thank-yous." He looked as if he had been made an unwilling conspirator, trapped into aiding and abetting criminals whom he abhorred. Linda and Heidi stood by the counter. By any standards they were very pretty girls. This morning, their color high and their eyes excited and dancing with the thought of the ransom for their friends that had arrived, they looked radiant. I leaned against the tobacco counter and watched the young clerk. What did he see when he looked at them, I wondered. His pale blue eyes were flat and opaque. It was the look I had seen on the faces of New Yorkers as they stepped around a sick drunk who lay inert on the steps of the subway station. It turned inward, away from the offending stench, shutting out the sight with a flick of the lid.

Sheriff Hollowell counted the money carefully. Methodically, he totaled the amounts once again and filled in the proper forms.

"Get the girls," he said to the deputy. We heard him scraping on the steps as he trotted upstairs. Moments later, the girls filed into the room.

The sheriff turned from Dale, who had been handling the bail trans-action, and nodded toward the girls. His voice was neutral. "Have any of you been mistreated here in any way?"

George Winter, Ione, California.

The girls shook their heads in the negative. Their faces showed the strain of the day in Drew and the night in the Indianola jail, but they looked unharmed.

Hallowell turned back to Dale. "I'll notify Moorhead that you're coming. You can take the girls now."

Gretchen stretched her arms in the sunlight of the street and lifted her face to examine the tiny window on the second floor of the jail. "That's where they put Ellie and me," she said. "Man, even in jail they segregate."

The segregated quarters had not really separated them from the Negro girls. They had called to each other, and late into the night they had sung together.

Ellie pushed a strand of hair from her forehead. "Ugh! Do I need a bath! Let's get the boys and go home."

The long, low buildings of the county farm lay sweltering, blanketed in the sodden heat of noon. A Negro "trusty," in the wide stripes of his prison suit, stretched flat on a bench in the sun. The striped chest rose and fell, and the nasal snoring sounded gently in the hushed glare. The blue-black skin shone with sweat, one dark wrist and hand dangling limply to touch the red turf. The jailer stepped outside to watch our cars move into the yard. His narrow shoulders hunched against the brightness, and the deep shadowed eyes looked ferociously from the tight ferret face. "You just stop. Right there!" He spat on the lifeless sod of the drive. The spare, bent figure crossed the yard without another glance, and disappeared into another low building. The prone prisoner continued to sleep, and the snoring sawed the silence.

Ten minutes later, the boys stepped from the building. They looked exhausted and filthy. Squinting in the blinding light, they climbed into the cars. I reached back and pulled the door closed.

"Are you all right?" I asked.

Jeff Sacher, looking pale and ill, grinned weakly as he settled into the back seat. "We're all right. It's just that I'm allergic to the straw or something in that sty. My eyes and nose are running. I'll be fine once we're out of here."

Jim Dann nodded. "Let's get out of here."

I started the motor, and the prisoner in the yard sat up, startled. Jim waved at the man as we wheeled past. "That poor guy has been here nine months." He glanced at Jeff. "Imagine. Nine months in this place."

The prisoner straddled the bench, his large hands bearing all his weight as he leaned forward to watch our cars move down the road to the gate.

"He tossed cigarettes to us over the fence," said Jim.

The striped figure never moved. It shrank in the rearview mirror, and was gone.

The white boys had shared one section, the Negro boys another. But the heat and the rank, nauseating offal of waste and despair were democratically parceled out. A drainage ditch near the screenless windows sent clouds of insects into the odorous cells. "It was a menagerie," said one of the boys. "We had lice, mice, chiggers, mosquitoes, flies, and the skins of two snakes that had once lived there."

Angry welts of bites and scratching covered the visible skin of most of the boys. Jeff Sacher's eyes were puffy and inflamed. His voice was alert and vibrant, but his eyes streamed and tears trickled down the caked cheeks. "It was just so damn dirty. And so damn hot! For a while that jailer kept a fan going, and it helped a little. But late last night a call came through from Senator Keating's office, in Washington. Keating wanted the local authorities to know that he knew one of his constituents was being held in Moorhead. The jailer was sore as hell, and he turned off the fan."

A Negro youngster from Drew leaned forward from the seat near the door. He laughed and shook his head admiringly. "You should have seen McLaurin," he chuckled.

I caught McLaurin's eye in the mirror. He looked unruffled and fit. "What did you do, Mac?" I asked.

"I didn't do anything," he smiled. "I just curled up on the cot. The kids kept askin' 'When are we gonna get out?' and I couldn't tell 'em because I didn't know. So I curled up on the cot and slept. All the time I was there I just slept."

20

Perhaps it is the breezes that blow down the broad reaches of the Mississippi River as it slides majestically past Greenville. Maybe they bear a soft breath of other places into the town. Or perhaps it is the river itself, moving swiftly between the leveed banks with its people and cargoes from Chicago and St. Louis and New Orleans. One feels a difference in Greenville, subtle but real, that separates it from the rest of the state. The visitor notes with surprise that the local paper is liberal, edited by outspoken Hodding Carter. It is successful and influential. The stultifying provincialism that infects the newspapers of the state, even those in the one large city, Jackson, is missing in this small metropolis of thirty thousand. Like the river, Carter's paper speaks of other places and other ways. Its influence on the manners and morals of the community have graced the reputation of the town. In a state where rampant racism is either practiced or condoned, Greenville remains a small island of genteel sanity.

The morning I drove John Harris, Fred Miller, and Charles McLaurin to the Federal Courthouse in Greenville, we moved slowly along the shaded avenues.

Fred Miller, the young Negro Freedom School teacher from Prichard, Alabama, admired the handsome homes.

"What's Greenville like, Mac?" he asked.

"It's a good town. A real good town. In Greenville you don't get beaten by the police when you get arrested." McLaurin's voice carried no note of irony. "I'd rather get arrested in Greenville than any town in Mississippi," he said with conviction.

John Harris,
Howard University.

What an accolade, I thought. They ought to print it on the "Welcome" signs. "Welcome to Greenville. We don't beat Negroes when we arrest them."

The COFO lawyers had succeeded in changing the jurisdiction of the arrest cases from Drew. Once McLaurin, Harris, and Miller had signed the removal petitions at the courthouse, all twenty-three cases would be moved from the municipal court in Drew to the calendar of a Federal judge. The chances of winning in Federal court were good, and we were delighted at the developments. We were greeted at the office of the clerk of the Federal District Court by the two white lawyers who had arrived from Jackson. They busied themselves with the endless copies, and had the boys sign each page of the removal petitions in the presence of the clerk. In twenty minutes, the chore completed, we left the office with the lawyers.

"Let's have a good lunch," I said. "With drinks! We've got something to celebrate!"

Maynard Omerberg, the lawyer from California, pointed to the corner. "About three blocks from that corner is the Downtown Motor Hotel. Supposed to be the best place in town. I understand it's been tested since the Civil Rights Bill was passed and that they served Negroes. Shall we try it?"

McLaurin shrugged. "It's okay with me. It ought to be good." He smiled, remembering. "They chased us away last year when we tried to go in."

The restaurant of the motor hotel was "motel-modern." It looked inviting, and the air conditioning would be a welcome relief from the midday heat. It was noisy and bustling with the lunch trade of downtown Greenville. We filed into the restaurant and stood for a moment next to the door. The clatter of silver and the chatter of conversation ceased as if on signal. I looked quickly about, seeking a table for six. Finding none, I led the way to an empty table for four. The two lawyers searched for two chairs to pull up to our table.

The three young Negroes and I took our seats. Out of the corner of my eye I saw the manager. He stood behind the cashier's desk, his face flushed and angry. With relief, I noted that he picked up a handful of menus. He started across the hushed restaurant toward our table. Very carefully, he placed menus in front of McLaurin, Miller, and Harris. He straightened up and stepped back. His voice sounded unnaturally loud in the quiet room. "*You* will not be served here."

His face paled, and his eyes were locked on mine.

"I beg your pardon?" I asked, not yet understanding.

The blood had rushed back to his face, mysteriously released by the sound of his own voice. "I said, *you* will not be served here."

I had a great impulse to laugh aloud at the apoplectic manager, but Omerberg, standing behind him, shook his head briefly. "Okay, let's go."

We all rose from the table and followed the lawyers to the cashier's desk. The manager had regained his composure. When the California lawyer asked for his card, he replied, "Certainly," and handed it to him politely. The voice was once again calm and suave. His eyes flicked across the six of us, and returned to the lawyer. "We will be happy to serve you when you come back in separate parties."

As we pushed open the door, the cheerful hum of lunch conversation renewed and followed us to the street.

We contained ourselves only that far when the pathetic absurdity of the situation insisted on release. We all exploded in laughter.

"I'm sorry, fellows," I said. "If it wasn't for me, Mac, you could have made it this time!"

I called home that night from Mrs. Hamer's living room. "Honey," I said, "about this discrimination. We've had it all wrong. It's *whites* they won't serve in Mississippi!"

21

Summer moved across the Delta. The gentle rhythms of waking and working, eating and praying had become familiar. The dwarf cotton plants recorded the passage of days and weeks. They ripened and stretched, seeking the golden apple of sun. Dirt caked in the fields but was hidden by the myriad leaves that now touched row on row. The sight of dusty students had ceased to be remarkable to white Ruleville, and the passage of the police truck with the pacing dog through the Quarter occasioned hardly a glance from the Negroes or the students. The reality of the "invasion" had finally caught up with the fear and exaggeration of the white community's anticipation. Wholesale defiance of segregated facilities had not taken place. The work in the Freedom Schools continued, and the caravans down to the Indianola Courthouse had become routine. The tempo of activity in the Negro community built quietly and surely as the summer moved into August.

The white community watched and waited. If the hysterical trepidation of the early days of July had flown, it had been replaced by an uneasy speculation. Soon the summer would be done. What was to happen when the students returned to the campus?

There were some clues.

Though the voter registration drive had yielded few new voters, it was clear that the pressure on the registrars of Sunflower County was going to be ever more insistent. Federal suits against registrars in other counties had torn the screen of systematic denial. When given the same opportunity to qualify as the Mississippi white, the Negro had been quick to register. If he had not known before, he learned at the Freedom School that juries were picked from the voting lists. "Without Negroes on those lists, can you get justice in Sunflower County?" The ride to the courthouse at Indianola became an act of faith.

If white Ruleville was alert, it noted that the teams of workers moving through Negro Ruleville were increasingly comprised of Negro teen-agers. The kids at the Freedom School were reading books and asking hard questions. "How come our teachers at the high school 'Tom' for Mr. Charlie, and don't register to vote?" Their voices were angry, and there was talk now of strikes in the fall if the teachers wouldn't go down and try to register at Indianola.

The Negro principal at the high school found his office increasingly occupied by students and lawyers from the Project, and they, too, were asking hard questions. "Is it true that whole classes of Negro students go out to pick cotton during the harvest? Is it true that the money earned goes to the school, and not to the boys and girls? Is it true that there is no accounting made of the money earned and what it is used for?" By August, the principal had begged Mayor Dorrough for police assistance in keeping unwanted visitors from his school. A current of protest throbbed just below the surface. The white establishment and its Negro mercenaries felt the vibrations and waited fretfully for the summer and the interlopers to be gone.

Early in August it was learned that the "Summer Project" was to carry through the fall and winter, and ambitious plans for a larger "Summer Project" were being debated for the next year. Some of the students would not be returning to campus. They would stay on in the community centers and Freedom Schools. White Mississippians watched and muttered in frustration. So long as the students stayed, they knew they would have to continue to put up with the swarms of press, network, Justice Department, and FBI people that had flooded their state since spring.

The façade of the white community remained as monolithic in August as it had been in June. If there were strains of passion or conscience within the structure, they were fraternal secrets. The façade remained intact. The overt hostility of fire and violence had been replaced by the passive intransigence of the sheriffs and the police. The white face we had learned to know so well remained unmoved and unchanged. It was full of loathing and hate.

We remained in a kind of social "no man's land," quarantined from any contact with the Mississippi white. The prohibition against mixing with us was rigid and absolute. The night a middle-aged white business-man came to the community center to satisfy his curiosity and argue the merits of segregation, he was arrested by Ruleville police and taken to jail. The shocked students phoned both Mayor Dorrough and the FBI to seek the segregationist's release. We wondered what the businessman's family and friends were thinking as "social quarantine" of the "outsiders" became jail for one of their own.

A short block south of the Indianola Courthouse a cluster of poor bars and down-at-the-heel cafés marked the beginning of the Negro sec-tion of town. Beyond stretched the residential neighborhoods of Negro homes. Some resembled the worn shacks in Shaw, but more were small and neat like the modest homes of Ruleville. Laced throughout the dusty, sun-filled blocks of this larger town were the homes of the small Negro middle class. Though they resembled exactly the homes of the neighboring whites in adjacent blocks, in these rows of poor people's homes they were conspicuous by their relative affluence.

Perhaps a mile and a half from the courthouse, beyond the homes and the Negro high school, was the Negro Baptist School. It stood naked in the midst of beanfields. A dirt driveway arced prettily from the road to the steps of the porch and continued its sweep back to the macadam. The brick building faced the road from a distance of about seventy yards.

McLaurin sat in the front seat of my Chevy and stared at the school and the fields. He opened the door and walked slowly up the steps to the porch, measuring the distance to the street with an appraising eye. I followed him inside. Two small lavatories led left and right from the front door. The rest of the space was one long, narrow room. Windows in the rear opened on the glare of the fields. McLaurin had heard that the school was not being used, and, sight unseen, had persuaded the Baptists to let him use it. He looked at his prize now with a smile and opened his arms. "It's not only great," he said. "It's brick!"

For weeks, tentative probes by the students had prepared the ground for the real push in Indianola. Gretchen Schwarz, Charley Scattergood, and John Harris had quietly moved into the community. They had been delighted by the quick response they had found, particularly among the high-school students. One outdoor meeting had been held, without fanfare, in a driving rainstorm two weeks before, and the youngsters' excitement had been unquenchable. "Where have you people been?" one of the Indianola kids had asked. "We've been waitin' and waitin'!"

Now that the school was secured, a force of students from Ruleville came to work with the three who were already there. George Winter had prepared leaflets, and they were distributed by the students and the local youngsters to every Negro home in Indianola. "Mass meeting at the Baptist School tonight!" was the word, and it sped from block to block.

Rabbi Al Levine from Rochester, New York, had joined us in Ruleville a few days before. He was the third succeeding chaplain to have been assigned to our group. Unlike his two predecessors, he was a veteran of the civil rights struggle in Mississippi. In 1961 he had been a member of the first ministerial Freedom Ride that had moved south through Georgia and Alabama, ending in Jackson, Mississippi. Levine made it clear immediately upon his arrival in Ruleville that he wished to be considered a participant as well as a spiritual counselor. Now that the crucial meeting in Indianola was about to be held, he drove to the Baptist School with Chuck Adair, the Protestant clergyman he was replacing. I met them on the porch early in the afternoon. Levine puffed morosely on a large-bowled pipe. His rounded sloping shoulders and sad hound's eyes gave him a melancholy air. "I'm worried about tonight," he said.

I burst out laughing. "*You're* worried! *Everybody's* worried. Indianola is the birthplace of the White Citizens Councils, and nobody thinks they're going to sit still for this. McLaurin told me this morning that he doesn't think that more than a few local Negroes will dare show up at a civil rights meeting."

Levine's pipe had gone out, and he busied himself with relighting it. His teeth clenched on the yellow stem, and his eyes sought mine over the flaring flame of the match. He drew on the pipe till a cloud of smoke billowed from the great bowl, and he waved it aside impatiently. "Come with Chuck and me," he said. "We're going to pay a clerical visit on the chief of police."

The small, chatty police chief had been pleasant enough. He was quick to agree with Levine that with women and children in the building, we should try to avoid any trouble. He promised police protection "within

the capacity of our small force." Levine had thanked him and requested that they remain outside. "To discourage any intruders on the meeting, chief. We don't need policemen inside," said Levine, "just outside."

The chief had nodded agreement. "They'll be outside, rabbi. I don't expect any trouble."

We were still arranging benches and chairs in the hall when the first kids began to drift into the yard from the surrounding neighborhoods. By seven o'clock, groups of teen-agers and young women were crossing the yard from the street, their heads bobbing animatedly. By seven-thirty, the entire hall was packed with an exuberant and expectant crowd of two hundred and fifty. The walls were lined with people who could not find seats, and clusters of children leaned in every window. The elderly sat scattered through the crowd, their eyes bright with excitement and wonder. For the first time in the summer, I noticed a large group of the middle-aged. Husbands and wives, some with tiny children in their arms, chatted quietly, waiting for the meeting to begin.

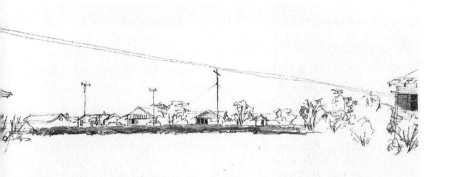

The Community Center and Freedom School in Indianola.

John Harris leaned against the wall at the front of the room. "McLaurin's on the way from Ruleville," he said. "Probably driving like mad!" He looked out at the hundreds of Negroes that filled the room and grinned. "I hope I can see his face when he walks in!"

The sun had fled from the beanfields, and lights were beginning to shine in the houses beyond the fields. The high Delta sky was lavender with dusk as Harris flicked on the naked bulbs in the school and moved to the front of the room. McLaurin came across the porch and made his way slowly through the noisy congestion at the door. His dark glasses swept the crowd. He was shaking his head as he made his way around the packed benches to stand next to me against the wall. Harris had seen him, and with a wide grin led the crowd into song. They responded with a rush of sound, and the exultant voices lifted in unison:

> *Black and white together,*
> *We shall not be moved.*

McLaurin's eyes were wet and he grinned like a foolish Buddha. His fist rubbed the end of his nose, and he wagged his head in joyous disbelief. As the song swept the hall, his voice sounded harsh and shaken in my ear. "Man! This is *Indianola*! Do you *realize* that? *Indianola*!" His voice broke and his face shone with pleasure. "I thought there'd be ten people here! Look at them! In *Indianola*!"

For McLaurin it was the happiest, most incredible moment since he entered the Movement. Five times he had been jailed in this town! Here, now, was the reality of every fantasy he had dreamed during the lonely, frightened nights in the Delta. His tough, compact body moved with the powerful urgency of the words.

Just like a tree that's planted by the waters,
We shall not be moved.

John Harris let the song subside. He sensed that the familiar music had eased the strangeness that always accompanied a first meeting. His boyish face was smiling, and he nodded approval to the eager faces. "I'm going to introduce you to one of the persons who has been leading the freedom fight here in Mississippi for..." the voice stopped abruptly. An angry murmur had started near the door. Harris resumed, his voice uncertain. "Well," he said, "we've got an unwanted guest in here."

People rose from their seats and benches scraped shrilly on the wooden floor as the crowd strained to see. A woman next to me whispered along the row, "It's Slim!" An alarmed cry sounded and was repeated around the hall. "Slim! It's Slim!"

McLaurin moved swiftly along the wall toward the huge Negro policeman who had shouldered his way into the center of the room.

I touched the arm of the woman who had first spread the word. Her frightened eyes swung toward me.

"Tell me," I said fast. "Who is Slim?"

Her chin rose, and her eyes were angry and black. "He's a killer. He's killed two Negroes."

An ox of a man with a heavy, dull face and enormous hands, Slim stood like an animal at bay. His jaw was lowered, and the eyes stared furiously at Al Levine who blocked his path. The noise was shrill in the hall, and Levine's quiet voice was drowned in the surging sound. McLaurin reached the rabbi's side as he was repeating slowly what he had already said. As if to a slow child, Levine patiently explained that police were not needed or wanted inside. "Don't you understand? The chief promised us that the police would stay outside."

The policeman's eyes seemed not to comprehend, and the great hulk stood as if rooted to the floor. McLaurin's voice rasped through the excited babble. "This is church property. You have no right to be here."

Slim's yellow eyes shifted from the rabbi to McLaurin, and they narrowed in recognition. His thick neck strained at the blue collar, and one heavy hand moved slowly to rest on the holster. The oxen slab of face was shining from the steamy heat of the room. The small eyes studied McLaurin. Silence had suddenly surrounded the two men. Slim's voice could be heard clearly. "I'm stayin' right here."

McLaurin turned and pushed his way through the agitated crowd to the front of the heaving room. The nervous whispering ceased as he raised his hand for attention. The short, chunky body balanced on the balls of his feet, and his whole attitude was taut and controlled. Ignoring the policeman, he addressed the back seats and benches of the room. "Before we start here, I'd like for you to know that this is church property. We've got an agreement with the police chief that says we don't have to put up with any policeman inside. But one has come in. Now, it's up to you whether you want him here or not."

Feet scraped on the floor as everyone stood, and a wave of noise roared through the long room. "GO! GO! GO!" The children had frightened half-smiles on their faces, but they screamed the word louder and louder. "GO!" It seemed that every throat in the crowd was unleashing its accompaniment to the barrage of sound that assaulted the policeman. I watched the fury on the faces of the old men and women. They were yelling "GO!" to a Mississippi policeman for the first time. They cut the air with a word they had never before said aloud. "GO! GO! GO! GO!"

McLaurin fought his way through the stamping, chanting crowd to the side of Levine. Slim's eyes were wide and staring as the crescendo of noise broke about him. McLaurin pointed to the door, and his vibrant voice scissored through the din. "YOU GOT TO GO!"

The policeman's great head rolled and his tongue licked at the heavy, lower lip. He stared at McLaurin. "I could kill you!" he growled, and heaved the heavy service revolver from his holster. As the crowd eddied about the tableau, someone saw the dull glint of the forty-five that was leveled at the rabbi and screamed. Slim stood transfixed. His eyes were frightened now, as the shouting, lurching crowd pushed from the rear.

White-helmeted policemen elbowed their way past the entrance and into the tense and throbbing room. A moment later they had wrestled the sweating, humiliated Slim through the crowd and onto the porch. The cries from the room followed them. "GO! GO! GO!" And now there was derisive laughter as well. Tomorrow every Negro child in Indianola would know that bully cop had been faced down.

McLaurin edged to the front of the hall. As he made his way clear of the milling people, he was greeted by applause and relieved laughter. He stood, face alight with excitement, waiting for silence. Slowly, the aroused crowd settled back on the benches and the seats. Slim stood just beyond the open doors, on the porch. The light spilled across the enraged face and touched the white helmets of the Indianola police as they clustered in the dark beyond the step. Police cars crowded in the arc of the drive, their revolving lights throwing shafts of red across the yard.

Levine's face was wet as he spoke rapidly to me on the porch. "I want to report this to the FBI. If a cop can pull a gun on the clergy, what will he do to someone like McLaurin?" With Chuck Adair, he moved down the steps and approached the police chief. The chief and Sheriff Hollowell separated themselves from a group of helmeted police and met them in the center of the lawn. Even in the crimson reflection of the circling lights, Levine's fleshy face looked damp and pale. A tremor in his voice betrayed his fatigue and tension.

"Chief, I want to call the FBI. Will you furnish me police escort to the nearest phone?" Before the chief could reply, the sheriff interceded. He stared at Levine, and called me over from where I stood watching in the darkness. "What happened in there, Tracy?"

I stepped into the group. "A policeman entered the school in the middle of the meeting. We had been told by the chief here that no police would come inside. The cop was told this and asked to leave by the rabbi. He wouldn't go, and everybody got pretty excited. I think he thought he was going to be jumped, and he panicked. He pulled his gun on the rabbi."

Hallowell nodded and turned back to Levine. "You can make your call from my office. Get in my car and I'll drive you down. You'll have protection with me."

As the rabbi opened the door of the sheriff's car, Hallowell slid in on the opposite side. The dashboard light flashed on his face, and he looked carefully at the rabbi. His voice was neutral and flat. "It's not right for a minister to be frightened."

Levine closed the door and returned the sheriff's even look. "I'm not used to having a policeman stick a gun in my belly," he replied simply.

Chuck Adair climbed in the back, and the car ground into gear. It edged past the prowl cars and wheeled down the drive.

I entered the school and made my way along the wall. Through the window I could see the red eyes of the police cars spin in the dark. The metallic chatter of the car radios sounded lifeless and lonely. In the long, hushed room, McLaurin's voice sounded almost conversational. "I'm not unmindful tonight that many of you are here against the will of your folk. Kids are here against the will of their parents. Women here against the will of their husbands. And many men here against the will of their wives. And I understand why they were all against your comin'. People have been killed in Mississippi for comin' to a Freedom Meeting! But I know that something's happening, something's changing. For better than two years we've been trying to get a meeting in this town so the people of Indianola could say out loud—in public—what they've said over the years as they crouched under their beds, prayin'. Say out loud that they were tired of bein' pushed in corners. Tired of the way they were living. Tired of havin' Mr. Charlie tell them when to move, how to move, and where to go! But now something's changing. You're not askin' Mr. Charlie when and where and how. You're *here*—tonight—attending a Freedom Meeting! In Indianola!"

He swallowed hard, and there was a timbre to the voice as it rang out. "To me, this is a *great* thing. A *great* thing!"

His eyes were shining with his pride in them. He gestured toward the door where the huge policeman moved restlessly. His voice was ripe with scorn, and he hurled his words at the glowering man who ceased his pacing back and forth to listen.

"I'm not unmindful of the fact that right here in your city you have a policeman who should be pickin' cotton!"

The silent tension was torn with hooting shouts and screams of laughter. The faces were full of contempt and mocking.

"Not unmindful," he cried, "that right here in your city you have a policeman who is not qualified to be a policeman!"

Two police mounted the porch and stood with Slim, staring at McLaurin. McLaurin's voice fell, inviting the confidence of the rapt crowd. They strained forward to hear.

"You know," he said almost casually, "Once when I was arrested up in Leflore County, a white official told me something. He said, 'If a white policeman shoots a Negro, you have a racial crisis. But if a Negro policeman shoots a Negro, you don't have a racial crisis.'" He stopped, and every eye moved to the door. For a long moment there was complete silence in the room, and the brittle murmur of the police radios could be heard. Then McLaurin's throaty voice spat the words: "And that's why they hired Slim!"

A single breath seemed to suck through the audience, and then was expelled in a sighing "YES! Oh, YES! YES!" It repeated and soared "YES!"

"We own this country as much as anybody else." Charles McLaurin in Indianola.

A roar seemed to fill the space, a wild mixture of relief, laughter, scorn, and admiration. Tears stood in the eyes of the oldsters, unbelieving half-smiles on the lined faces. They watched this boy—this David—come to battle. And they cried.

When the room quieted again, McLaurin shifted his tack. Never again did he so much as glance at the policemen near the exit. His voice was full and he spoke with confidence.

"For years I've known that we aren't the scary type of people. Our ancestors killed lions! They ate the meat of animals that could tear men apart! We're the same people that fought on foreign soil in two world wars and in Korea! We're not afraid!

"We weren't afraid to go over there and shoot people who never did the things to us that these white people in Mississippi have. We weren't afraid!"

He stood motionless, searching the wide-eyed faces of the youngsters who bunched along the walls. Softly, he asked the question. "Then why don't we shoot the white folks here?" The voice stopped again, and he took a half-step closer to the teen-agers. His voice spoke softly to them, and their heads nodded gently. "Because in this movement we don't hate. We love. Because in this movement we are going to win by being nonviolent. Because even in Mississippi we're Americans. Born here. Raised here. That soil out there is enriched with the tears, the blood, the bones, and the sweat of our ancestors. We own this country as much as anybody else. America is sacred to us. America is a land that we want to live in."

I think often of that meeting in Indianola. In a way it seems a microcosm of the whole Mississippi summer. All the elements were in that room that night. The barely suppressed violence of the police; the thrilling awakening of a people who for a hundred years had known only the nightmarish sleep of the hunted; the bone-tired, dusty kids from the campus, who knew that something private and profound had been stirred deep in them, altering them forever. And the young Mississippi Negroes, like McLaurin, making themselves *say* it, making themselves *do* it, making themselves be brave for all of us.

McLaurin's voice had been vibrant with hope and full of the wonder of the moment. He had leaned toward the children and his young voice was joyous. "What's happening today is *real*. Not something you're reading about. It's happening right *here*! *You* are doing things that people before you would not have dreamed of doing. You are *here*! You won't say 'I heard it.' Or 'somebody told me.' You'll say: 'I was *right there*! I *saw it*! My *feet* were in that place when history was *made*!'"

Part III
REPRISE—MISSISSIPPI 1965

22

One forty-six. *Choonk!* One forty-seven. *Choonk!* One forty-eight. *Choonk!* The insistent whack of the hoe hitting the ground stopped, and the sudden silence made me open my eyes, blinking at the bright rectangle of light that shone on the ceiling. The angry rattle of pebbles being flung by the flailing hoe had pried itself into my slumber, and I had lain in the soft lap of the bed—counting. One hundred and forty-eight! Like a steam drill the chopper had methodically and unsparingly moved down the garden outside the window. I stretched across the bed and pushed the patched cotton curtain aside, squinting in the six-o'clock brightness to spy the John Henry with the hoe. The skinny, leathery figure of the old lady who lived next door to the Williams' stood alone in the dewy garden. Legs straight and slightly parted, she stooped to snatch the roots of the weeds from the freshly chopped earth. The hoe lay still on the ground as her hands moved swiftly in the dark furrow. Minutes passed, but the rhythm of the bent figure's toil continued swift and sure. The spindly legs seemed rooted, the bony frame effortlessly bent at the waist. The face was lost in the shadow of the shapeless straw, and ragged scraps of gray hair were matted on the shining surface of the mahogany neck. Suddenly, with the grace of a twenty-year-old, she rose, the hoe extending athwart the row of snap beans. Once more the blade sliced into the green skein of chickweed, dandelion, and grass. The ancient arms resumed their tireless assault on the rich soil of the Delta. *Choonk! Choonk! Choonk!*

I let the curtain go and lay back on the bed, marveling that a whole

Old farmer

year had gone since last I had been in this tiny room. My eyes played across the stained and weathered walls, seeking out change. The brown felt of Mr. Williams' old farm hat seemed grayer and dustier on its nail above the mirror. The wide brim curled at the edges, and a stain of red earth had long since dried on the crown. Like Mr. Williams, the hat seemed a gentle prisoner of the tiny house, a fragile memory of another time. Two of Sharon's dresses, one pink, one blue, hung from a hook beside the mirror. Last summer she had been only a brown, diapered doll!

One tiny white dress had been her costume for church. The dresses lay still against the ochre wall. No breeze stirred the fragile gauze of the crisp and ironed organdy.

"Sha-ron!" The raw edge of annoyance rode up the scale, the voice gusty and belligerent.

Sharon's squeal of tiny petulance cut through her grandmother's formidable roar. The old, rusty voice broke, giggled, and exploded in huge laughter. I heard the door from the Williams' bedroom open and the pat of bare feet move across the battered linoleum of the kitchen. Water pounded from the single tap into the percolator. I stretched luxuriantly on the bed, studying the patterns of sun on the ceiling. The *choonk* of the hoe moved past my window. I could feel a fine film of sweat forming on my bare chest. It was almost seven o'clock. I was back in Mississippi, and it was going to be a hot day.

Was it a weariness that I sensed as I moved through Jerusalem Quarter? I knew from Mrs. Williams' letters that the winter had been hard, that want and hunger had stalked the dwindling stocks of vegetables that had been put up last summer. The weather had been bitter, and cartons of clothes from the North had helped the community limp through the long months of no employment. Perhaps it seemed like weariness because only the old men and women and the youngest children were visible. The elderly sat on the tiny porches or panted gently in the warm shadows of the dusty trees. They nodded and smiled as I drove slowly by, and a few called "G'mornin!" softly. The quarter felt enervated, drained of vitality. I knew that the young and the physically able were off to plantations, chopping around the delicate shoots that feathered the dark Delta soil. Heat lay damp and heavy, and no vagrant zephyr moved the dust-shrouded wild grass along the road. Or was this the normal rhythm of the Negro community? The pulse of last summer had been vibrant, erratic—often staccato. At all hours the quarter had been so intensely alive! Like a besieged town, black Ruleville had inched its watchful way through the long days and nights of the summer. In its midst were the golden children from the North, come, incredibly, to do battle with segregation. They had moved eagerly into the hard lives of their hosts, bearing gifts of love and certainty. And for one blazing summer the sweet confidence of their spirit had illuminated for the Negro's believing eyes a brief vision of the possible. With meetings and classes and demonstrations there had been no time for weariness.

By summer's end, the students had left the Delta to return to college, to graduate school, to the family business. As they had swung their bags into the bus heading north on Route 41, they looked like the same fresh-faced kids who had arrived two months earlier. But in the crucible of the long, hot summer they had been subtly altered. If they had come to Mississippi with shapeless fears of physical peril, they left with the certain knowledge that in their country innocent citizens can be killed, arrested, spat upon, and reviled. Three of their own had been murdered. A year would pass after the broken bodies had been torn from their earthen grave, and still the state of Mississippi would fail to find them legally dead. No murder indictment would be drawn. No one tried. It was a lesson these strangers from the North would never forget or forgive. The reality of judicial perversion and kangaroo courts was a stunning, an awesome fact. It did violence to their sensibilities and their idealism. Their sudden vision of the deliberate corruption of the democratic process, of the immense distance that separated what we espouse from what we do, of the naked terror of being a pariah in your own land transformed their innocence cruelly.

They had withstood the tears and entreaties of their parents to come home. They had learned to live with their fears; to rise up frightened, to go to work frightened, to go to bed frightened—and to endure. If they had at first believed that courage alone could reshape a citadel of political power and economic privilege, they returned to campus that fall with a profound conviction that courage was not enough. Once back in school, they felt older and changed. They smarted with impatience and viewed their once-familiar milieu with sharp tongues and caustic comments when they found sham or pretense. To many of their old friends they seemed somehow strange and removed. For the returned veteran of Mississippi, it was a painful time of self-examination. For, like infantry back from the front lines, they lived with the gnawing guilt that they should never have left. As I drove slowly through Jerusalem Quarter, I wondered how many of them would be returning to the Rulevilles of Alabama, Arkansas, Mississippi.

Kids who had known me hollered greetings and waved as I turned the corner near the high school. Roy, half a head taller than last summer

Noon at the Sanctified Church in Ruleville.

when he would endlessly toss a softball against the roof of the house next door, appeared suddenly in my rear-view mirror. He trotted behind the car, grinning widely. I braked and he came shyly to the door. "Hi, Tracy!" The soft words and shining eyes were warm. "You want to throw a ball around?"

"Sure, Roy! But not right now. I'll see you at the house later."

A small addition was being constructed at the Negro high school. White carpenters shifted lumber as a ragged handful of Negro children scattered like sparrows across the tufted weeds of the playground playing tag. I slowed as I spotted an eighteen-year-old girl carrying a tiny infant in a flowered cotton wrapper. She had stepped from the doorstep of a small patched house that sat silhouetted against an immense cotton field beyond, and she paused to watch my car. She had been active in the youth group last summer, and I remembered her unquenchable humor during the tight moments of the arrests in Drew. She cocked her head and stared at the car. The slim, girlish figure moved closer, and then she recognized me. Her intelligent eyes crinkled and she broke into warm laughter. "For heaven's sakes! I thought you were a bill collector! When'd you get back?"

Her arms cradled the infant carefully, and she nuzzled the tiny brown face as she held the child for me to see. "This is my daughter, Tracy." Pride and love lit her young face. The worn, flowered cotton was spotless, and two somber black eyes watched me from the heart of the bouquet.

"She's beautiful, Marguerite," I laughed. "At least what I can see of her! Are you living here with your mother?"

She nodded, smoothing the wrapper away from the tiny chin of the baby. "Mama takes care of the baby when I go to chop." Her face was calm and unapologetic. She knew that, like so many other children in the quarter, her baby would grow up knowing its mother and its grandmother, probably never knowing its father. Few young Negro men in the Delta could assume the responsibilities of fatherhood on the wages they could earn, but the compulsions and urgency of youth could not be dissuaded. The result was a candid acceptance of love-making and its usual consequence. The Delta was filled with the offspring of coupling that was only sometimes given the legitimacy of marriage. I had heard it so often: "Are you kidding, man? On six hundred dollars a year? Get married? I'm cutting out for Chicago." Or Cleveland. Or Harlem. The women would stay, raising the children, waiting for the fare that would be coming someday from the North, knowing that it would be a miracle if it ever came. I looked at the bright, alert face that hovered lovingly over the tiny human package. Her eyes were still merry, as I remembered them, but they didn't look as though they ever expected miracles.

A clean and shiny sedan moved past us. It turned abruptly into the driveway of the comfortable, white, frame house that lay shaded by the maples in the schoolyard. A tall, slender Negro swung from the car and mounted the steps to the porch. Marguerite's eyes followed the figure of the high school principal until the screen door slammed. The tiny tip of her pink tongue moved along the full upper lip. She frowned, patting the tiny back of the infant that nestled against her shoulder. "Tom," she said. Her voice was flat and cold.

A gulf had grown between the aroused students and the frightened school administration which was trying to hold the line against change. Contempt by the students for the Negro arm of the Establishment had been the result. An attempt on the part of the authorities to bridge the gulf by abolishing the detested summer sessions brought no reconciliation. I sat motionless at the wheel after Marguerite had returned to the house, studying the principal's shiny sedan in my mirror. How terrible and sad a word. "Tom." She had spat it like a curse. When change would come to the Delta, I realized with a shock, it would not come from the educated, "safe" Negro who placed "accommodation" before freedom. It would come from the disinherited and the uneducated adults whose lives had been totally stripped of all but desperation. And it would come from the kids, thirsting for knowledge they now knew was there to be had—and for power that they were just beginning to understand.

23

Mayor Dorrough shoved the papers on the table top to the pale plump lady who managed his office. She clutched the papers and stepped quickly around me, disappearing through the door into the glare of the street. Rising, he turned to face me where I stood, just inside the front door. The sentinel face was unchanged by the year. The salt-and-pepper hair, a little long, seemed grayer. His chin was down, creasing the jowl that matched the small paunch of his stomach. His eyes were careful as he regarded me over his horn-rimmed glasses.

"Sugarman," he said.

I stepped toward him with my hand extended. "How are you, Mayor?"

He shook hands briefly and motioned me to a chair. He circled his desk and eased into his chair.

"I'm pleased you remembered me," I said, smiling. "It's been a whole year."

He grinned and pulled open his desk drawer. He lifted a sheaf of stapled newspaper clippings and waved them next to his ear. "Oh, I keep up with you." His eyes were smiling, but his mouth was tight.

I squinted across the desk and recognized that the top clipping was from my home-town newspaper. It was a news story about our fund-raising efforts for a community center in Ruleville. His grin spread as he watched me.

"Yeah. People send me things, and I manage to know something about you."

"Well, that's fine. They we don't have to talk about me," I said. "I don't know a thing about you! I've come down to see what's been happening in Ruleville over the year."

A smile played across the large pink face. "A citizen up your way wrote this office that 'a damn Jew was coming down here with four thousand dollars for the center.'"

I laughed. "He was wrong, Mayor. It's six thousand dollars! People up home have been working hard."

He shifted in his chair, stooping to open a drawer. He took out a sub-division map of Ruleville and opened it flat on the desk. "You'll be interested in this." His finger pointed out the land that had been acquired for the center. "They want to build here."

"I know," I said. "I hope you're pleased about it. They need it. It should be good for the town."

"They can do anything they want. I'm not against it. But look here." One finger rested on the acquired land as his other hand swept across the town expanse. "This land they have is a far spot from most of the Negro community. The people in Boston who are raising money for the center wrote me, asking me to check that their money is not going to go down a rathole. I think a center should be closer to the heart of the Negro community." His finger moved to the cotton field that lay alongside the main highway that crossed Ruleville from east to west. "This land is adjacent to the Negro high school. I think I could get the town to acquire it and swap land with the center people. Don't you agree it would be a better location?" He leaned back and brushed his hair with the back of his hand.

"I can see your point, Mayor. But, of course, I don't have anything to do with it. That's the business of the Ruleville Community Center Trust. I think you ought to talk with some of the officers of the center. After all, they raised nine hundred dollars for that land among the folks in the quarter. We outsiders are just trying to help them get a building up."

He wrinkled his nose in annoyance. "I talked to Foster who lives in the quarter. He said that they weren't interested in swapping land. So I thought I would bring it to your attention."

I shrugged. "I'm afraid you'll have to discuss it directly with Linda Davis, Mr. McDonald, or Charles McLaurin. They're the officers." I leaned toward the map and put my finger on the highway. "I don't know, but I suspect that their objection is one of security. At your location, they'll be vulnerable to any redneck who drives by and decides to heave a gasoline bottle. The site they've picked for the center is only a couple of blocks away, and it's a dead-end road." I glanced at Dorrough. "After all, Mayor, that's a real consideration. It's happened in Mississippi. The Indianola Community Center was burned to the ground last fall."

The flush on Dorrough's face deepened. He scratched his chin and nodded slightly. "That's true, of course," he said. "But we've been able to hold that element down in this area. It's not a problem here." His voice rose. "We haven't let it become one, either!"

"You had a cross burned on your lawn last fall," I said. "I read about it in the papers in New York. I'm sorry."

"That's so. And poison-pen letters, too." His eyes clouded and he cleared his throat abruptly. "But that's a very small element. Very small. I'd say that at least two-thirds of this town—white and colored—are prepared to go along with the Movement now."

"What Movement?" I asked cautiously.

"The Movement in civil rights. The Federal programs. Look here." His finger moved along the roads in the Negro sections of Ruleville. Each had been marked with a red pencil. The rest of the town roads were marked in blue. "The red-penciled roads indicate the project we're hoping to get started; paving those dirt roads, adding sewers and curbs."

His pencil stabbed the Sanctified Quarter on the map and his voice was intense. "That quarter provided only about twenty-two hundred dollars in tax revenue. The road program for them will cost about sixty-five thousand. Without outside help from Washington, it would take thirty years to pay for it."

"If those folks had been educated properly and given some skills, you'd be getting a hell of a lot more than twenty-tow hundred in taxes, Mayor," I said, softly.

He tossed the pencil on the map and rocked back in his chair. The heavy brows met in a dark line as he studied his glasses, wiping them carefully with a large, white handkerchief. "We inherited a lot of problems. We didn't invent 'em all." His voice was caustic. "You know you can make a good case that the Negro has been an albatross around the neck of the South, holding us back all these years."

"He didn't ask to come, Mayor," I said.

"That's so." He shifted his bulk in the chair. The thick fingers gestured with the shining glasses. "I'll tell you something." The belligerent jaw tightened and the words were staccato. "I'm going after those Federal funds." The glasses perched once more between the bushy brows. His large head swung toward the empty brightness of the noon street. His voice was musing and soft in the empty room. "Next week I'm going to be sitting next to Governor Johnson at a conference. I'm going to speak—and then he's going to speak." He leaned forward, the head hunched into his neck. The big hands were clasped. His gaze returned to the room, and he struck his hands softly on the desk. "I'm going to put some things in that speech." He paused. "I'm going to ask that every single state law that opposes the Federal law be changed. Every last one!"

I watched the large fingers unclasp and start to fold the municipal map. I studied his face as he slipped the map into the desk. He glanced up and caught my eye. "I've been away, Sugarman. Working on plans for an urban renewal program for Ruleville. It calls for low-cost Federal housing units—apartments—to replace the substandard housing in the quarter. It's going to be hard. Ninety-five percent of those folks live on land that they or their relatives own. You know what some of the houses are like. That Freedom House isn't fit to live in—particularly in the winter. A lot of those houses should have been condemned and torn down years ago. But those folks have so little income that I'm not sure they can afford to rent at any price." His voice was bitter. "Just wait. If we get an urban renewal program into Ruleville, McLaurin will be hollering that we're grabbing up the poor Negro's property!"

"Don't write off McLaurin, Mayor," I said. "He's giving the good young people a reason to stay and help solve the problems here. McLaurin's going to college now—and so will some of these kids in the quarter." I studied the heavy face across the desk. "They may even help save Mississippi."

He snorted and stood up abruptly. "In five years McLaurin will have his degree and make some money." The cool eyes never blinked. "And then he'll move out of the Negro neighborhood."

"You think so?" I asked. "My bet is that in five years he'll be in the Mississippi legislature."

I followed him into the bright street, waiting as he carefully locked the door. As we shook hands at the corner, his husky voice was almost gentle.

"I'll say this. I think a lot of us in this state wish we had done some things differently. Some of us wish we hadn't said what we said. Or said it differently. I've got grandsons…." He paused, and his eyes moved absently across the deserted shimmering intersection. "It's hard to change … everything … all at once." His voice growled and the alert eyes snapped, squinting in the heat. "But the train is pulling out. You either got to get on it or get left."

24

"If Dorrough could honestly see what it is I'm after, he wouldn't feel like he feels about me."

I looked up, startled by the curiously forlorn note in the deep voice. Fannie Lou Hamer, her face wet and shining with perspiration, sat in the shade of the pecan tree in her front yard. She paused, and the cranky voices of crickets thummed in the skill, sun-washed air. We sat together, too drained by the heat to raise our voices. A year had passed since last we sat here together. The frame house seemed wearier. Perhaps it was the contrast. Last summer it had echoed to the racket of young people. The screen door of the sagging porch had seemed then to be constantly in motion. The unoiled spring would complain like a soul in torment, and the door would bang against the warped frame. Last summer the Hamer house had been the terminus for all the frantic activity. It seemed then that the typewriters on the porch and in the kitchen were always clacking, the phone always ringing. The tiny yard had always been alive with people. Now we sat alone, and the house drowsed in the afternoon sun. Paint had baked and curled back from the weathered wood, leaving splintered feathers of white in the dusty garden. Here in the deep shade of the pecan, the color of the zinnias was vibrant, mocking the painful white light that simmered in the quarter. I squinted at the heavy, damp figure of Mrs. Hamer. Her face in repose was melancholy. How curious, I thought, that Mayor Dorrough's opinion should sadden or even matter to her.

In the year that had passed, Fannie Lou Hamer had become a national figure. Mississippi Negroes, denied since Reconstruction from the deliberations of the Democratic party in their state, had formed the Freedom Democratic party in 1964. Claiming that the regular delegation to the Democratic National Convention did not truly represent all Mississippians, they had mounted a challenge before the Credentials Committee in

Mrs. Fannie Lou Hamer instructing voter applicants.

Atlantic City, asking that their party's delegates be seated as the legal representatives of their state. To seasoned political observers, the move had seemed quixotic and doomed to quick dismissal on the altar of party unity. But the searing testimony of Fannie Lou Hamer had been so stunning that the "challenge" suddenly became the exciting story of the convention. Throughout the nation, men and women sat riveted to their television screens, compelled and deeply moved by the testimony of this untutored woman from the Delta. The recital of her sadistic beating by Mississippi police tore the veil that conceals the brutality of life in the South. For many Americans it was their first appalling confrontation with the calculated savagery of white supremacy. Calls and telegrams poured into the convention, and the delegates were stirred to a historic decision. Two members of the Freedom Democratic party were invited to be seated with the regular delegation, and for the first time in history, a major party pledged to refuse in the future to honor any delegation that had not been democratically chosen. The fact that both delegations had refused to be seated would be merely an odd footnote in history. But the precedent for the future had been established. The Freedom Democratic party had become a political reality. Fannie Lou Hamer was its symbol and its spokesman.

For a year now, like a tireless Jeremiah, she had mounted the pulpits and platforms in the great cities of the North. "Righteousness exalts a nation," she would cry, "but sin is a reproach to any people." She would move awkwardly across the stage, limping from the polio-stiffened leg. The strangely moving voice, so elemental in its directness and passion, would fill the auditorium:

> *To tell it on the mountain...*
> *Over the hills ... and everywhere...*
> *Go tell it on the mountain...*
> *To let my people go...*

I watched her now, panting slightly in the oppressive heat. The yellowish eyes were sad. She shook her head. "But Dorrough can't see." The voice was like a mirror of her emotions—moving like quicksilver from sadness to mirth to irony. It lifted now, shading delicately from sorrow to anger. "It's strange. It's not just Dorrough. So *many* white people down here can only see one thing. And they think that one thing is involved in everything we Negroes want and do. And that's 'sex'!" The screen door whined open, and her daughter Virgie skipped down the steps. Smiling shyly, she settled on Mrs. Hamer's bench, curling comfortably against her mother. Mrs. Hamer's hand touched the neatly braided head and settled affectionately on her daughter's delicate shoulder. Her eyes, that had softened at Virgie's appearance, clouded. "We're not thinkin' about *sex*, Tracy. Man, if we can get somethin' fair for what we do, get our kids in a decent school so they can get a decent education ... that's all." She shook her head in despairing wonder. "But all they see is 'sex'!" The voice was exasperated, frustrated by the blindness of "those that would not see." "You know the kinds of friendships that were built down here last summer between the students and the folks in the quarter. We'll never, under heaven, forget them. And they'll never forget us. And it's not for *sexual* reasons!"

Mr. McDonald's dusty truck bumped its way up the road. A brown arm waved from the cab as it passed. Mrs. Hamer grinned and raised her arm. "Hi, Mr. Mac!"

I nodded at the receding truck and smiled. "I was just thinking how different it seems now," I said. "Last summer when a pick-up truck would turn down there at the corner, we'd all start sweating!"

Mrs. Hamer nodded. Her eyes narrowed, and she watched the dust settle in the hollows of the dirt road.

"We've gone through a whole lot of suffering in Sunflower County, and last summer those students suffered with us. But you're right. It is different now." She paused. "Virgie, get us a cold bottle of water from the icebox." She watched the slender twelve-year-old trot across the lawn and mount the porch steps. When she spoke again, her voice was level and low. "I believe now that if anything were going to happen to me—and I'm not saying it's *not* going to happen—it would happen outside of Sunflower County. Sunflower is just not as bad as it used to be, although we still have Drew to deal with! But even in Drew, which is like South Africa, they followed me from house to house when I was up there workin' on registration for the Freedom Democratic party—but they didn't arrest me."

Virgie reappeared with glasses and a bottle of cold water. She placed them next to her mother on the bench. "I'm goin' on down to Martha's house, Mama." The voice was low and musical.

"Okay, honey. Pap will be home soon, and we'll make supper when it gets a little cooler." She silently handed me a glass and we sipped the cool water.

It was Sunday, and Virgie's sweet singing filled the car.

It isn't nice to block the doorways
It isn't nice to go to ja-il...

Mrs. Hamer's rich contralto sounded like a soft pedal in an organ, moving strongly beneath the child's tender voice, like a mother's hand. I hummed the song and grinned. What Mayor Dorrough of the future would have to cope with Virgie Hamer? The car accelerated as we left Cleveland, heading south in the Delta toward Greenville. Mrs. Hamer had been invited to speak at a church service that afternoon, and I had offered to be her chauffeur. Winds buffeted the car, sweeping clouds of dust from the baked fields. They tumbled and danced, tan smears against the lowering sky. I felt the wheel tug against the force of the gusts.

"Rain! Come on, rain!" chanted Mrs. Hamer. "Rain on the Andrews plantation!"

I laughed. Only a week before, a hundred people, the families of members of the Mississippi Freedom Labor Union, had been thrown off the Andrews plantation in Washington County. The union members, who had twice before requested a dollar twenty-five per hour, confronted Andrews at five-thirty on the morning of May 31, and informed him that they were striking. He had responded by summoning the police, ordering the families off the plantation, and dumping their household goods along the highway. It was the beginning of a struggle that would continue in the weeks and months ahead.

I had first heard of the strike on the very afternoon I arrived back in Mississippi. Two work-shirted youngsters placing colored pins in a wall map had looked curiously at me as I entered the Freedom Democratic party headquarters in Jackson. A third was speaking excitedly into a phone.

"Tractor drivers! Yeah. You're sure they were tractor drivers? Great! We'll check you later." He scribbled on a pad and called across to the others. "Five tractor drivers in Indianola are out."

As he hurried across the room to the map, the boy noticed me for the first time. "Can I help you?" he asked shortly.

When I told him I was headed back to the Delta after a year and was simply "reporting in," he leaned against the battered desk and smiled.

"We don't have the same security setup as last summer. It really isn't necessary. If you've got Mississippi plates on your car, that's enough. You should have no problems." He had handed me a form to fill out stating where I would be staying "for the records." When I had finished, I joined the three young men at the map. The area near Shaw held clusters of pins. Pins at Tribbett, a few at Cleveland. A scattering of pins at Indianola.

"What do they mean?" I had asked.

"Blue pins stand for cotton choppers, white pins for truck drivers, and red pins for tractor drivers who have walked off their plantations," one of them said.

I had stared at him. "What do you mean 'walked off?' On *strike*?"

He had nodded. "On strike." He had waved his hand at the Delta. "Almost a thousand of them. And it looks like it's just starting."

"But are they organized? They'll get clobbered if they're not organized. Do they have a union?"

He had nodded again. "They organized it in Shaw. Months ago, before the planting began. They call it the Mississippi Freedom Labor Union."

Now a week had passed. As we drove through Shaw, I pointed to a field beside the highway. A white family, mother, father, and children, were chopping between the long rows of cotton. No Negro laborer was in sight. The family never looked up, but intently pursued the weeds that were threatening the fledgling crop. Dust swirled about them as the wind whipped across the black tableland. The first drops stained my dust-coated windshield.

"Come on, rain! Rain for the strikers!" Mrs. Hamer cocked her eye at the black sky. "If it rains good, those weeds are going to multiply. Come on, rain!"

The sky cracked, and a ragged sliver of lightening lit the road as we passed from Bolivar into Washington County.

"You must have a direct line upstairs, Mrs. Hamer!" I laughed. "Here it comes!"

I slowed the Chevvy as the rain beat against the car. In seconds, the hollows between the rows of green were awash.

"It's only right," said Mrs. Hamer with satisfaction. "Those people've got guts, and they need all the help they can get."

"The Mississippi Freedom Labor Union is going to have a tough time organizing," I said. "The last strike down here was in the early thirties, and it was broken fast. Do you think the Union should be a part of the Freedom Democratic party?" I asked. Her expressive face became thoughtful.

"No," she said slowly. "I don't think so. I think anything the FDP can do toward helping the union keep going is important. But the union should be kept separate. After all, the FDP was organized because people couldn't have anything to say in the government. The union was organized because people couldn't get paid fair for what they were doin'. This union will give thousands of folks the chance to say: 'We want more for our work, or we're not gonna do it.' And that's somethin' that we've wanted to say all our lives!" The large face turned to watch the water cascading in the fields. She grinned and tapped Virgie's knee with pleasure. "Oh, my! Look at it rain!"

Finally, the rain had slackened and we rolled down the windows of the car. A freshet of rain-fragrant air poured in. Mrs. Hamer's spirits were bubbling. "It's catchin' on, Tracy! Oh, I think this union will spread more and more! Five hundred people have walked off here in Washington County alone. Last week it was only eighty! It's catchin' on because *folks* are catchin' on. Even in areas where we civil rights workers have never even been! They're goin' out on strike because they're tired. Tired! And it's reasonable enough, because I know how tired you get when you work from sun to sun for three dollars."

We moved down the glistening ribbon of road. It rolled south as straight as a ruler edge. In the distance I saw the first cluster of motels and gas stations that preceded the entrance to Greenville.

"It seems to me, Mrs. Hamer, that there are an awful lot of people who will see the union as more of a real answer to their problems than the Freedom Democratic party," I said. "After all, take-home pay must seem more important than a vote to lots of people down here who have never voted."

Mrs. Hamer hitched forward in the back seat and leaned her great arms on the backrest beside my shoulder. The rich voice was low and intense. "At first. Maybe at first. But once those folks come off the plantation on strike, they'll find out what's goin' on. They want to know! They've found the strength to walk out on strike because they're hungry for something! When we in the Freedom Democratic party tell them what the vote *means*, what that vote can do in support of their fight against the Man for a livin' wage, there'll be a whole lot of people in the rural areas who never cared about voting before that are goin' to become registered voters." Her voice was buoyant and confident.

I wheeled sharply in front of the church where she was scheduled to speak. As I pulled on the brake, I turned to grin at her. "It's amazing to me, Mrs. Hamer. In *one* year you've had the birth of the Freedom Democratic party, the congressional challenge, the Voting Rights Bill—and now, the Mississippi Freedom Labor Union!" I shook my head. "Everything is new!"

The great brown face shone with pleasure. She tapped my arm and her smile widened. She nodded. "*Everything! Everything* is new—and all of it is *great!*"

25

"Come the day after tommorra'," she had said on the phone. "We'll have coffee on the patio. And you can meet our new son, Jan. He arrived in November." I had wondered how she would sound. At Christmas I had sent them my card, a sketch of white and Negro children racing across a meadow, and I had speculated about their reaction. The voice was warm. "We got your card at Christmas, and we certainly appreciated hearing from you." I smiled. Noncommittal, but not hostile. "Come about ten."

Allison led me through the new sunken living room. Two masons were chipping bricks for the raised Bermuda fireplace, oblivious to our passage across the room. "Did you notice I'm using Negro workmen?" she whispered. Her impudent grin lit her sunburned face, and she tossed her blond hair as she led me onto the new patio. The year that had passed had done nothing to harness the irrepressible qualities of Allison Cutler. She seemed, if anything, younger and more vibrant.

"Look who's here," she said, nodding toward the two men who rose to greet us.

Billy Cutler unfolded from the wicker chair with the gracelessness of

an overgrown boy. The fleshy neck and paunch were less visible once he rose to full height. He was as I had remembered him, perhaps a bit thicker in the waist. He held out his hand and smiled. "Glad to see you again, Tracy. Meet Steve Perkins."

A slim man in his late thirties stood smiling at Cutler's side. Though the day was overcast, he squinted from the glare. Skin crinkled attractively around his eyes, and the mouth was humorous and sensitive. He stepped forward, his head slightly extended in a frank and searching sweep of my face. "I'm happy to meet you," he said in a gentle voice.

Two nights before, in Mrs. Williams' kitchen, Olivia Waters had discussed her boss, Mr. Perkins. "You ought to go meet him, Tracy," she said vehemently. "He's from Colorado and he's a fine man. He's no hater. You'd like him. He's a good friend of Mr. and Mrs. Cutler."

"Olivia," I had said, "You know I can't just go ring a white stranger's doorbell in Ruleville. After all, I've been *invited* to the Cutlers!"

She had nodded, folding her heavy arms across the white uniformed expanse of her bosom. "I know. But it's a shame. You two would get on."

Now, as I took Perkins' hand, I recalled James Baldwin's remark: "We Negroes know all about you, but you don't know anything about us. After all, we work in your kitchens and you've never even seen ours." I felt excited at being secretly armed by Olivia Waters' kitchen intelligence. In the still, moist air of the patio the four of us carefully sipped our coffee.

The conversation moved lazily through the heavy air, the easy bantering of old friends. The three had recently returned from a holiday to Yucatan, a celebration of the birth of young Jan. "Steven is the only person in the whole world who could persuade Billy Cutler to fly away from Ruleville on a vacation," purred Allison. She fondled the memories of the trip like an excited child. Her eyes flashed, and an evil grin lit her expressive face. "Steve had told me that when we got to Yucatan I should respond to any question in Spanish (which I do *not* understand—not one single word!) by saying 'No, no, no.' I'll tell you," she giggled, "one look at those Latin men and I decided to say 'Si, si, si!'"

Perkins' shoulders shook with silent laughter. He was hunched over his coffee, relishing the story. Billy mopped his neck with a moist handkerchief, his narrowed eyes restlessly moving across the great expanse of sky.

"It's damp as hell," he muttered, "but not a real rain in three weeks." He walked past the baby's playpen to the end of the patio and rolled a huge fan onto the flagstones. It roared in the background as we hitched our chairs closer to be heard. Billy leaned forward, the thick arms making small, damp stains on his khaki pants. "What do you think about this Mississippi Freedom Labor Union, Tracy?"

"Oh, no," groaned Allison. "I want to talk about Yucatan!"

"I never heard about the union till the other day," I said. "What do you think?"

"Damn, damn, damn," muttered Allison and went to tend the waking baby.

Perkins stirred his coffee, listening attentively. Billy's eyes were bright. The face that had seemed so indolent in repose now was alert. He leaned forward and snapped off the fan. In the sudden silence his voice sounded unnaturally loud.

"A dollar twenty-five an hour is going to hurt the niggers. Hurt them bad. In the end they'll be the ones to suffer. The plantation owners will have to let two-thirds of them go if they insist on that kind of money." He tapped my knee. "Take my place. I've got more tenant families than most around here. Almost thirty. If I have to pay a dollar and a quarter, I'll have to run twenty of them off my land. I'd hate like hell to do it, too." The wicker chair creaked as he leaned back, surveying the pearl brightness of the overcast sky. "What's going to happen to those families? Just forget them? Let them starve to death?" His chin dropped to his chest and his troubled eyes sought mine. "I've known most of those folks all my life."

"I don't know the answer," I said. "Maybe the government will have to subsidize people like they subsidize cotton, Billy. Come in and teach these people modern skills. Hasn't automation been pushing the Negroes off the land, anyhow?"

Perkins, nodding quietly, set his coffee down. "That's true. The Delta towns have become way-stations North for the people being automated out of their jobs. This union thing is going to speed up the process." He relit his pipe and smiled at me over the flame. "In a conservative magazine that I am sure you would not approve of, I just finished reading an analysis of the problem the world faces trying to feed an exploding population. I assure you that within fifteen years the crisis will be very real. We're going to have to become very much more productive as farmers. My farm is a regular stop for U.S. State Department tours for visiting agricultural people from all over the world. Every week there are visitors from Ghana and Pakistan and Poland, and they're all looking for answers on how to speed up farm production. One of the answers, of course, is that stoop labor on the farm must be replaced with more efficient means. It's going to have to disappear if the world is going to grow enough to feed and clothe itself during the next decades." He tapped out the pipe and sucked absently on the stem. "The old plantation system created a monster of cheap, unskilled labor. It worked then. But it's got to go now or it will strangle the South."

Allison and Billy had listened attentively. I realized that Perkins had tacitly been made their spokesman. Articulate and well educated, he spoke also with the authority of one who had proved himself a success in his sixteen years in Mississippi. A year before, Billy Cutler had struggled to explain and defend his point of view during our long afternoon together. Apologizing for his own limitations, he had nevertheless attempted to transmit honestly his worries at the prospect of the Mississippi Negro gaining the vote. Those concerns, I suddenly realized, were not even being mentioned now. Though unspoken, I now sensed an acceptance—albeit reluctant—of the growing enfranchisement of the Negro. It was no longer "whether I would allow my niggers to vote." It was now a concern that in their organized strength this new force could strike at his economic sinecure. This frightened him. Cutler was struggling to adjust to a landscape that had suddenly—violently—been tilted. The old touchstones and shibboleths were scattered—inexorably pushed aside by the churning current of his time. Goldwater's disastrous defeat; the realization that Goodman, Schwerner, and Chaney had indeed been murdered; the inexplicable tenacity of the Texan in the White House who had dared trumpet on national television: "We shall overcome"—all had conspired to make him feel alien to his time. He struggled to keep his footing in this newly strange place, and he looked for help from people like Perkins, for his was one of the voices of the New South. It was quiet, controlled, and pragmatic. It spoke of the future, not the past. And it was urbane. It echoed a world that reached far beyond Billy Cutler's Sunflower County.

When Perkins invited me home for lunch, I accepted gratefully, pleased to have the chance to talk further with this thoughtful man. Allison shook hands at the door as we left. Her eyes mirrored the annoyance she felt that the conversation had moved to talk of the Delta.

"I wish we had time to *really* talk … about skiing resorts, and travel, and New York. It seems that in Ruleville we never get to talk about interesting things like that. We talk about small-town things—about whether the rain is going to come in time for the planting—and about each other. My, don't folks here love to talk about each other!" She brushed back a stray lock of hair and her eyes became mischievous. "If they run out of things to talk about, I just walk to the Rexall Drug Store in short shorts and they start all over again!"

It was not till we were approaching Perkins' home that I remembered Olivia Waters. I watched Perkins from the corner of my eye. "I have a small confession to make, Steve," I said. He wheeled the car into the driveway and under the overhang by the side door. He snapped off the ignition and turned his head to listen, his eyes curious.

"A confession?"

"You weren't really a stranger when we met this morning. I had heard about you from your housekeeper, Mrs. Waters."

"No kidding! From Olivia! Well, I'll be darned!" He laughed with delight. "Won't she be surprised!"

"It was all good," I hastened to add. "She seems to approve of you. She hoped we'd have a chance to meet."

"Oh, Olivia's a fine woman. She keeps my body and soul together!" He chuckled as we climbed from the car. He opened the door and held it for me as I stepped into the large, cool, and unfashionable rooms of the old house. He nodded toward the brightly flowered slipcovers of the living room furniture and made a face. "It's not very chic and not even my own sorry taste. I rent this place furnished." He crossed to the hall and stuck his head around the door leading to the kitchen. "Olivia, come see who our guest is for lunch."

The round, composed face appeared in the doorway. Her eyes widened and she beamed. A huge grin lighted her face. "Well, now! Mr. Sugarman! Now isn't that nice!" The bright eyes moved swiftly from Perkins to me and back to her employer. "I told Mr. Sugarman about you." The words were unadorned and unapologetic. The affection beneath the words was accepted and understood. She wiped her hands on her apron. "I'll go fix lunch."

Though modest in speech, Perkins' pride in his cotton operation was obvious as he moved about his office. With great enthusiasm, he explained the organization of his nine hundred acres. Full-color photographs of planting, of snowy harvest, of green vistas that stretched to the Delta horizon, of combines, of tractors were spread before me like a family album.

"The plantation looks beautiful," I said, "particularly at harvest time."

He nodded. "It is. It's not the Kodachrome!" He scooped up the pictures and slid them across the top of his desk. Turning, I was struck by the sudden seriousness of his expression. He balanced himself against the edge of the desk. "But it's not a plantation. It's a farm. I dislike the word 'plantation.'" The distinction seemed to be very important to him, as if the acknowledgment would somehow make him vulnerable. "It's just a farm. A damn good one, too." His face suddenly smiled. "Even though my friends, the Cutlers, call me a 'gentleman farmer' to kid me, I'm not. I work too hard for that!"

Luncheon was served by a smiling Olivia, and Perkins was a gracious and relaxed host. The shining china and cut flowers on the spacious table seemed to be a thousand light-years removed from the moist heat and clutter of Mrs. Williams' kitchen. Olivia moved happily back and forth from the kitchen, treating me with the deference paid an honored guest. I felt, somehow, a guilty sense of betrayal. It was too easy, just too easy. For the first time in Mississippi, I felt disoriented as I moved from one world to the other.

It began, finally, to rain as we settled to talk in the living room after lunch.

"Billy finally got his rain," I said.

He nodded, stuffing his pipe. "I never realized how important weather was till I started farming here sixteen years ago." He smiled. "You might say it's our favorite subject of conversation."

"Steve," I said, "you've lived most of your life away from here. Your perspective is a different one from Billy's. What is it that keeps these people so out of step with the consensus of the country? Is it the local radio? The TV? The newspapers? What keeps them from knowing the score?"

He shook his head and frowned. "I disagree with your premise. You assume that they're unsophisticated because they refuse to join the national consensus. You think that they're prisoners of their local radios and local papers. You think that they don't really know what's going on. You're wrong. They get the news. From magazines, from letters, from their kids in the service, even from a lot of television that comes into the state. No. In some ways they're the most politically savvy people I've ever met. It's not that they don't know the score." His eyes were cool and candid. "It's that they don't *like* the score."

26

Linda Davis's gentle voice had been hushed with sadness. "It was terrible. The staff was demoralized. We all watched it happening, helpless and miserable. When word came in May that McLaurin was coming back from school to head up the project, some of us cried with relief."

Bitterness and dissension had grown like a rank weed in Indianola. Springing from frustration in the unnatural heat of a besieged fort, it had all but destroyed the staff during the bleak months of the fall and winter. Personalities had become unbearably abrasive. There seemed to be no way of healing the thousand tiny wounds that bedeviled the sensibilities. They had been inflicted during the days and nights of the arrests that followed the picketing of the public library; the destruction by fire of the community center that had been so cherished; the beatings in Moorhead and Inverness; the bombings that had leveled the homes in Indianola. The fury, that had been fed by the faceless destroyers and arrogant police, rose like hateful bile. Having no natural release, it turned inside. It seized on petty alliances and suspected ambitions, alienating friends and robbing the vitality that had marked the promise of last summer's beginning.

If the staff was shaken and exhausted, McLaurin was not. He returned from Mississippi Valley State bursting with energy. I watched him move now into the divided ranks in Indianola, the quiet strength of his personality asserting itself modestly but surely. There was no dramatic confronta-

"I used to be so scared when I first came to work for SNCC in the Delta."
Charles McLaurin, project leader.

tion or showdown. McLaurin had confessed to me that he considered leadership to be showmanship, and like a sensitive actor he had a sure instinct when to command the stage by movement and when to be still. He was aware of the anger and the distrust that had throttled the young leaders of the project. Instead of ministering to their bruised feelings or dramatically attempting to "rally the troops" with appeals to their idealism and loyalty, he set to work on programs of action that would demand all of their youthful energies.

"They're not going to have time to brood," he told me. "In a week this program is going to be rolling, and there's going to be just too much to do."

He had been right. The emotionally drained staff had turned gratefully to the work ahead.

An excitement seemed to churn inside McLaurin. You could read it in the bounce of his walk, hear it in his vibrant voice. He seemed extraordinarily alive. Last summer he had been hidden deep within himself. The sunglasses had been his moat. Only when you came very close and glimpsed the wide-open eyes behind his dark glasses did you sense the humming energy bottled within. He had been a well-insulated dynamo. Only at the public meetings had that energy become kinetic, galvanizing action, illuminating the possible. But now he was exploding with plans and stratagems for the summer ahead. The dark glasses would perch precariously high on his brow as he would crouch over a table, hammering out his ideas. As the glasses would start to slide down his forehead, he would brush them back impatiently. The year at college seemed to have armed him, and he was eager to fire every arrow *now! At once! Yesterday!* How far he had come, I thought. And how fast.

The second night after my return to the Delta, I sat with McLaurin in one of the tiny, uncomfortable booths in Amzie Moore's grill. The small space was a bedlam of noise. A techni-colored jukebox all but filled one side of the steaming room, the salmon, orange, and lemon colors turning endlessly deep within the bowels of the vibrating monster.

Hit the road, Jack,
And don't ya' come back no more, no more, no more…

The sound of Ray Charles, amplified fully, competed with the laughter and chatter of the young voices.

Hit the road, Jack…

The girl from behind the counter placed the pint of bourbon and a bowl of rapidly melting ice cubes on the edge of our table. Her eyes were on McLaurin's face, and she smiled coquettishly. "Anything else, Mac?"

He nodded. "Yeah. Two hamburgers. What do you want with your bourbon?" he asked me.

"Soda," I said.

He grinned. "Naw. You can't get soda in here. They don't know what soda is! Two Cokes," he said to the girl. He rested one arm on the back of the low booth and poured the bourbon on the ice in his glass. He chuckled. "I have to laugh. My wife's friends from college think I'm really 'way out' because I drink soda with my scotch at our house! 'Where'd you learn to drink that way, Mr. McLaurin?'" he mimicked. "I tell 'em in New York, Washington, and Los Angeles!" We laughed together.

"What this *Mister McLaurin* jazz? Gloria's friends really call you *Mister McLaurin*?" I asked.

He grinned over his glass and nodded. "They really do!" He took a swallow and put down the glass. "I think they're afraid of me because I don't 'small-talk.' They're old friends of Gloria. From high school, most of them. They call her 'duck.' But they call me 'Mr. McLaurin!' 'Mr. McLaurin!'" He hooted, shaking his head, for he knew how short a time he had felt sure of himself.

"I used to be so scared when I first came to work for Snick in the Delta. I'll never forget the first day I got three old ladies—Mrs. Williams was one of them—to agree finally to go to the courthouse in Indianola! These ladies were from fifty to eighty, and I was wishin' that there were some younger people goin' who could give *me* courage! It felt so strange. You ask people to go to the courthouse, and you tell them that they should and that there's nothin' to be afraid of. And you're so afraid yourself!"

The waitress leaned across the narrow counter. "Here you are, Mac!" she chirped. He reached from the booth and took the Cokes and the hamburgers with barely a nod. The girl wiped her hands on her apron and smiled happily at McLaurin's back. It was not the first time I had noticed the strong attraction that Mac's masculinity had for the girls. They moved to be close to him, to be noticed, to be available. McLaurin would keep aloof, laughing, "playing it cool," talking about his wife, but somehow never quite disqualifying himself from their attention.

He hunched forward, eager to continue his reminiscence. "I was shakin' before we ever left Ruleville, and when we passed that service station on the highway where the white fellows were known to beat up Negroes, I got down in that car seat as low as I could get!" He swallowed a bite of hamburger and shook his head, smiling. "As we drove, the old ladies were talkin' to each other, but I wasn't sayin' a thing. I acted as if I was interested in watchin' the folks workin' in the fields along the highway. But, really, I just didn't want those old ladies to hear the tremblin' in my voice!" He laughed at the memory, and his eyes seemed to be reliving the scene. "When we finally got to the outskirts of Indianola, I felt I had to say *something* if I was going to overcome enough fear at least to tell the Man in the registrar's office what we wanted! So I started to talk to Mrs. Williams a little, and then a little bit more, and finally the shakiness in my voice started to pass. When we finally reached the courthouse, I just didn't want to get out of the car, but those old ladies ... soon as we stopped ... were out of the car and movin' up the steps!" He shook his head in wonder. "I sat there, tryin' to figure out why it was that all these years people had been sayin' that the folks in the Delta were afraid to register, afraid to voice. And here I was—younger, stronger—a registered voter who had had no trouble registering in Jackson—and I was hangin' back while those three old ladies were walkin' right up to the Man and tellin' him what they wanted! I finally followed them up the stairs, just waiting for someone to grab me!" He paused, remembering, and when he spoke again his voice was warm with affection. "I'll never forget those old ladies. Never. They were my beginning. That's when I started to become a man."

Our little table was a constant target of shouted greetings from the men who moved in and out of the grill, and of the smiling attention by the girls who perched near the counter or crowded around the small tables.

McLaurin lit a cigar and settled back in his seat, cradling the glass of bourbon. He seemed completely at ease, oblivious of the pounding rock and roll which beat through the small room. He talked about his year at college. It had been no retreat or sanctuary from the real world, though his involvement with the Movement had, of necessity, been curtailed. Mississippi Valley State had been a place where a man could get the things he needed to know, the historic perspective he needed to acquire. "Why, man," he exclaimed, "the Movement in Mississippi is the new Populism!"

He had swallowed books and ideas whole, discovering a world of parallels and contradictions that he had never suspected existed. His eager mind sought to understand and make the abstractions relevant.

"I've been reading all kinds of books. Books on government, Richard Wright, Galbraith, Ellison, books on politics, all the essays of James Baldwin. All kinds of books. I'm not interested just in a 'balanced' book: these are the good points, these are the bad points, about Jimmy Hoffa, for instance. I'm interested in how did he do it, how did he make it happen." He swallowed deeply of the bourbon, and absently wiped the edge of his moustache with his forefinger. "I can read another book about Hoffa with another point of view. That's okay. Same with Dawson, Diggs, Adam Clayton Powell. I read a book called *The Negro Politician*, and I don't know if it was a good book or a bad book. But it told me things I wanted to find out." He put down his glass and laughed. "In a lot of ways I idolize that cat Powell."

"How can you, Mac?" I protested. "He's no statesman. He's a 'wheeler-dealer' politician."

He grinned. "Maybe *because* he's a wheeler-dealer politician!" The smile disappeared and he rubbed his mouth thoughtfully. "What's important about Powell is not that he's an operating politician. What's important is that he heads up one of the most important committees in Congress— Education and Labor."

"What about politics, Mac?" I asked. "We kidded about it last summer. A lot of things have happened since then. Is there a real possibility that you might run for public office?"

He studied the idealized Negro faces on the beer poster that hung over the jukebox, and he didn't answer immediately. "I've got to finish school first," he said finally. "Meanwhile I expect to stay very involved with the Freedom Democratic party in Sunflower County." He turned to look at me directly. "Yeah. It's a real possibility." His face lightened. "You know, I hate to go to parties. Gloria's always tryin' to get me to go, and I'm always sayin' 'no.' I told her the other night that even if I ran for the State Legislature, I wouldn't go to parties."

He smiled slyly, and lifted his glass. "But if I run for Congress, I'll go to parties!"

I laughed with him. "Any man that could face the police chief in Drew with confidence should be able to face his wife's friends at a party!" I looked at the cool young face across the table. When he wished, it disguised the inner man more completely than the dark glasses. "Level with me, Mac. *Were* you as confident last summer in Drew as you looked?"

"Yes." He nodded his head vigorously. "I was then. That was a whole year after that first trip to Indianola when I learned to hide my fear by talking. By the time you call came, I had been arrested four times in four different towns!" He grinned widely. "By then it was my mouth that was getting' me in trouble! When a policeman or a sheriff or a plantation owner would say: 'Don't do something,' there I'd be, tryin' to explain why we should! By sayin' something—by being 'uppity'—I was able to overcome my fear, even in the presence of large numbers of policemen. From 1963 I had started to move around the state, learning how to get around the danger spots anywhere in Mississippi, and especially learning all I could about Sunflower County. So by last summer I felt I knew all I should know and that I could take care of the people I was going to be bringin' back here with me from Oxford. At first I hadn't wanted the responsibility, and I told Bob Moses that some of those who wanted to come down to the Delta wouldn't last three hours, that a lot of them were goin' to get hurt. But Moses and Jim Forman talked me around, and I decided to work with the Summer Project when they said I could have my own group in Sunflower County." He paused, and his eyes softened. The voice was full of pride. "By then I felt like I owned Sunflower County, that it was mine. And not one person in my project was hurt all the time I was in charge."

I finished my drink and signaled the waitress for more ice and another pint. McLaurin looked relaxed and happy, tapping his glass gently on the edge of the scarred table to the beat of the music that never stopped.

"You look content, McLaurin," I said. "If you and Gloria have kids, would you want them to stay in Mississippi?"

He raised his eyes in surprise. "Yes." He said it quickly, instinctively. "Yes. I would." He frowned a little. "In spite of all the places I've gone, I always end up back here. I don't think I could spend more than two weeks away from Mississippi. I always get homesick. I'd want any kid of mine to be born here and raised here. And *educated* here," he added, emphatically.

"But *well* educated," I interjected.

He nodded solemnly. "Well educated. By the time my kids go to school in Mississippi, educational standards will be higher here. They'll be able to go to the better schools without trouble." He smiled. "People who have already started to push integration may well be around to see my kids actually walk in those doors they've opened!"

27

As I parked among the mud-spattered cars in the rutted yard, I saw Liz Fusco standing at the top of the church's wooden steps. The last I had heard of Liz indicated that she had remained at summer's end to coordinate the work of the Freedom Schools throughout the state. She was flushed with heat. The long braid of hair that tagged at her back and her bare feet gave her the appearance of a slim fifteen-year-old at summer camp. "Hey, Liz!" I yelled. She was startled; then she spotted me and waved a happy salute. It was a buoyant reunion made pleasanter still by its unexpectedness. I had come to Shaw to observe a workshop of the Mississippi Freedom Labor Union, and I had expected to know no one. Applause spilled from the worn, wooden building, and a murmur of voices could be heard through the open windows.

"Liz," I said, "meet me at the car when the meeting is over. There's so much I want to ask you!"

The workshop was informally but purposefully run by a young man of twenty. The hall was crowded with men and women of all ages. A sprinkling of children perched among the rows of wooden seats, and a number of attentive teen-agers crowded near the entrance and along the rear of the hall. As the moderator posed a question, hands were raised by people eager to testify. He selected the speaker by a nod of his head. The room was warm and hushed. It seemed more like a church meeting than a labor rally. The people strained to hear, silent and watchful. Only some of the old would interrupt with exclamations of "Yes! Oh, yes!" At the conclusion of each speech they would applaud enthusiastically. All that was being discussed had ceased to be abstract ten days before. These were the families on strike. Their language was ungrammatical, sprinkled with Biblical images, quaint to ears tuned to the careful cadence of educated speech. But the intensity of the intercourse of ideas, and the poignant frames of reference made the experience compelling. These were neighbors, exhorting each other to save their money for the lean weeks and months ahead. They were full of kindly and homely advice on how to shop, how to avoid being cheated by the peddlers and salesmen that could bleed them. They talked of a minimum hourly wage of a dollar twenty-five, of their fears of hospital bills that could destroy a family's last defenses, of how to petition for a Congressional hearing on farm labor and domestic help. As I looked at the intent faces in the shabby church, I thought that pioneers facing an

"You'd see mothers with babies in their laps at the Freedom School, and they were reading books like Freedom Road.*" Liz Fusco, Freedom School teacher.*

ominous future must have congregated like this, building their courage in concert from hidden mines of heart and spirit.

"I can eat fish," said an old man. "An' if they's no fish, I can eat berries." He smiled. "An' if they's no berries, I still got two teeth left to gnaw grass with."

After the meeting Liz met me at the door and we walked together across the baking yard.

"In Shaw! Of all places!" I said, indicating the unpainted, ramshackle houses that limped like aged cripples down both sides of the road from the church. "How did these people get to this point, Liz?"

She pursed her lips. "I don't know the 'how' exactly, but I'm not surprised it started here. It was up here in Shaw that I started to see what Freedom Schools really were, and they had very little to do with the organized 'book-learning' I had been involved in all summer!" She smiled wryly, and the bright, sparrow eyes were intense. "I started to see that what the people called the 'neighborhood meeting,' or the FDP precinct meeting, or *any* meeting where people began to really talk to each other was *Freedom School.*" She shoved her hands deep in the pockets of her blue jeans as she concentrated. A deep crease met the corner of her eyebrow, giving the young face a troubled air. "They weren't just school-agers— kids reading books." Her gaze moved to the church where people clustered about the entrance, speaking in small tight groups as they made their way slowly to the road. "One of the teachers down here last summer was a man named Morris Rubin. His feeling was that you educate kids by organizing them. 'You listen to them,' he'd say. 'You hear what *they* want, and then you deal with their problems where they are.' So he organized them, and they came alive." She paused and looked at me. "Late in the summer those Shaw kids held the first school boycott in the Delta."

We reached the car and sat gingerly on the overheated upholstery. Liz threw a slender, sunburned arm over the back of the seat and curled her bare feet under her as she continued her story. "Some whites in the Movement wanted to go over to the Negro school for a spaghetti dinner. When they got there, they were kicked out of the cafeteria. I guess that was the real beginning. Because then the kids boycotted the cafeteria, and then they boycotted the school. The authorities responded by closing down the whole summer session in the school. The kids got their parents behind them, and the question then was whether or not the parents would let their kids return to class in the fall without their demands being met. Well, there wasn't enough information or organization or statewide support to believe that they could win. So the kids went back to school." She paused, remembering. "The kids went back to school, but a community movement had begun. Adults and kids would sit together at FDP precinct meetings and talk about their problems—about leadership—about what they wanted. People kept saying that what they had to do was stay out of the fields and stick together. They began to implement the talk when forty of them signed a paper saying that when spring came they weren't going to go to the fields. People decided to plant gardens, live on fish. But most important, they decided that they weren't going back in the fields for three dollars a day. Not then. Not ever again." Her voice shook with emotion, and tears stood in unblinking eyes. "You'd see mothers with babies in their laps at the Freedom School, and they were reading books like *Freedom Road*. Her eyes moved outside to the lawn. Slowly the old cars were pulling away. Families walked along the road, kicking dust with their boots.

"What are you doing here, Liz?" I asked. "Are you involved with the union?"

She smiled. "No. I'm working with the staff in Greenwood. I just came to the workshop because I'm interested.

"It took me five months to learn, painfully, that you can't deal with education without dealing with people. And there I was, touring the state, distributing educational material to the Freedom Schools! Slowly, I began to realize that 'educational material' was not what the Freedom Schools were all about."

She hesitated, seeking the way to articulate adequately the process of change she had observed. But it was obvious that it had been a difficult concept to rationalize and accept. "You see, all of us who came down here last summer as teachers came down because we thought schooling was important. To us, in our own orientation, schooling meant classes where you worked with kids—helping them to read better, helping them to learn a little about who they were by giving them some American history and Negro history. A few of the kids we found who were particularly apt academically we even took back North with us at the end of the summer to get them into good schools. As teachers who had an abiding faith in education, we related best to those kids who seemed so eager to learn. But in the process we missed all those kids who were hostile to education, hostile to educated people like us, hostile to whites—the angry, revolutionary kids."

"I think you're being too tough on yourself, Liz. I don't think you can adequately measure the impact of the Freedom School classes on kids who had never before known a sympathetic white, let alone a trained and dedicated teacher. If you were missing the boat in connecting with the children, why didn't the project leaders stop the program?"

"They didn't," said Liz, "because most project directors last summer were intimidated by all us teachers with all our degrees and educational know-how. They didn't know how to say what they really felt about the Freedom Schools, but they had a general hostility for them which all of the teacher sensed. We thought it was because we were outsiders, moving into their territory. We thought it was jealousy." She sighed and shook her head. "But in the case of McLaurin, who understands the Movement, he was simply unable to tell us that we were going about it all wrong. So he withdrew and let me run the Freedom School ... and make a lot of mistakes. What's worst, of course, is that we lost contact with a lot of kids."

I nodded, remembering my conversations with McLaurin the previous summer. "Mac told me two weeks after the schools started last year that they could only be effective if the kids came to understand what the tools were for."

Liz listened attentively, her small, serious face nodding slightly. "I was torn between the teacher-types who were talking about 'remedial reading' and 'poor deprived kids,' and Mac's notion that you educated kids by helping them deal with their problems. Unfortunately, I didn't have enough communication then with Mac. He was with 'voter registration' and I was with 'Freedom Schools'...." She broke off with a weary shake of her head. "As if they could be divided! Well, this summer will be different."

I studied the young woman curled up on the seat. The childish slightness, the jeans and work shirt, the bare feet were deceptive. There was a burning dedication about her. You could read it in the bobbing thrust of the sharp face, the staccato drum of the thin voice, in the shadows that touched the bright, intelligent eyes.

"What now, Liz?" I asked gently. "Are you hopeful?"

She turned her wide eyes on me. "Hopeful? Oh, sure! What's happening all over Mississippi, what the kids and their parents have learned in a year, makes me hopeful." She stopped and turned her face swiftly away. A long moment passed, and when she turned again her eyes were dull. She looked for a moment like a sorrowing child. Her voice sounded small and forlorn in the still car. "But I'm damn lonely down here. All these programs are existing and I drop in on the, but I haven't *created* any of them—been the catalyst for any of them."

"What do you mean by 'catalyst,' Liz?"

She frowned, wetting her lips with her tongue. "Like Linda Davis," she said finally. "There's room for people like Linda who are catalysts in a community. She not only worked with little kids, she also trained people to work with little kids. People need this training, and down here they need it from people like Linda who care deeply about freedom." She thought for a moment. "You see, Linda doesn't *run* the community center. She doesn't *run* anything. What she does is ... be available. Available to sit down and talk with people about what it means to be qualified—and how to *get* qualified. Available to raise questions, and then to be content to let the people deal with those questions. But I'm an *organizer*, and I don't know if a white woman can do what an organizer *needs* to do down here—organize *men*. Maybe I'll have to go North—where I can organize whites. But I just don't know enough about organizing in cities to go North. I don't have the tools yet. At this stage I feel like I'm drifting, and I wonder how I'm to get the tools." The voice was delicate, hardly audible. She seemed almost to be thinking aloud. "Things are already going here. Shaw doesn't need me. Cleveland doesn't need me. Isaqueena County doesn't need me. Ruleville doesn't need me. Greenwood doesn't need me. None of these places need other people. And as a white woman—alone— I can't just go off and start to work in some rural town down here." She seemed suddenly impatient at the note of despondency that sounded in her voice. She sat erect and stared at the churchyard. It was empty now. A tiny muscle moved in her cheek. "I've been in Mississippi a year—and I've changed," she said slowly. "But I don't yet have the experience to evaluate that change."

28

Cephus Smith sat, self-consciously erect, in the front seat of my car. The lean, broad-shouldered nineteen-year-old looked straight ahead. A foolish plaid hat with a skinny brim was tipped low on his forehead, not quite shielding the late afternoon sun from his eyes. His skin was a burnt sienna brown that glistened in the warm light. I strained to listen, for his voice was at once husky and shy. "I'd never known any white kids before last summer. It meant somethin' to be around white kids—to be able to say what I wanted to say." He continued to stare through the dusty windshield at the disordered yard of the Ruleville Community Center. "It meant somethin' not to be afraid to say it."

I looked curiously at the young man. Try as I might, I could not really remember talking with him the summer before. He had been merely one of the pack of boys who moved on the periphery of the Movement. Tentatively poised at the back of a mass meeting in Williams Chapel, they seemed always ready for flight. Or lounging, elaborately relaxed, at the end of the Freedom School porch, one never quite knew if they belonged to the classes that met on the lawn. But somehow they were never *quite* out of earshot! They were boisterous as they played "rough tackle" on the parched dirt yard of the Sanctified Church next door. Hard-muscled bodies thudding against each other without protective equipment, their shouts of exuberant laughter splashed the summer air. They had moved around and about the center all summer, shy of the teachers, nudging and grinning at each other as they edged ever closer to the discussions on the lawn.

"I was sort of suspicious," said Cephus, "that they didn't mean what they were saying. It wasn't till after the summer—in September—that I got confident about the teachers. That was when Linda stayed here to run the community center alone. I was around and had nothin' else to do— I had graduated from the high school—so I'd drop around and do what I could. I knew Linda was goin' to need somebody around to keep it goin', so I'd drop around and lend a hand."

His voice dropped, and he shifted on the seat, frowning at the orange disk of sun that was framed in the center of the windshield. "I felt that white people like Linda, who had left their homes to come down here to work with us, needed someone here to work with them. So I decided to make her happy, make her feel like she was home."

He had run interference for Linda, easing the suspicions of some of the Negro community who wondered at the motives that would keep a young white girl working in that freezing farmhouse during the bone-chilling winter months. "And when the whites in town would cuss at her or say mean things," he said, "I'd be with her. I'd say: 'Just forget it. You hear it every day.' And she'd take it pretty good."

Through the long months of the winter and spring, he had become

deeply committed to the Freedom Democratic party. Working tirelessly with Linda and Mrs. Hamer on voter registration drives throughout the county, he was emulating McLaurin both in his involvement and his aspirations. "McLaurin is a good leader," he said firmly. "He and I are workin' together in the FDP now. Something has to change in Mississippi." New vistas of the possible had become apparent to him. "I'm goin' to Tougaloo in the fall," he said. "And then I'm goin' into politics. Sometimes I feel like stayin' in Ruleville just to challenge Mayor Dorrough." He grinned. "And sometimes I think I ought to challenge Governor Johnson!"

"You running for governor *already*, Cephus?" I laughed.

He shook his head and chuckled. "No. I'll start from the bottom of things."

The dry understatement made me peer closely at him. "Tell me," I urged, "what advice would you give a volunteer who was coming to work in the Delta?"

He looked at me for a long moment. "I'd tell him to be patient with the people." His voice was low, filled with tenderness. For the first time I realized how sensitive an organism lived inside the boyish figure in the absurd hat. His voice rumbled gently in the overheated car. "You have to be patient. When you talk with the people here about the Movement, give them time to think it over. Because people are easy to hurt."

The sun had dropped below the horizon, leaving a gaudy smear of rose and pink. It softened and suffused the fields and houses of the quarter. The air in the car was close, still but for a fly that bumped and buzzed against the rear window. "You have to give them time," Cephus continued quietly. "When they say 'Come back tomorra and I'll tell ya' what I think about it,' then wait till tomorra and go back to see them. There was a bad experience last spring. Some guys who were down from Tuskegee to work on the voter drive with us spoke to some folks in the street—askin' them to go down to the courthouse. When they wouldn't go, the guys from Tuskegee called them 'Uncle Toms.'" The young face winced at the memory. "Those folks were so hurt that they wouldn't even talk to *me*."

A tiny girl in a faded shirt moved out to the stoop of Mrs. Johnson's little grocery on the corner. She pulled the wrapper from a bright blue popsicle and let it flutter to the ground as she settled on the top step. She stared, unmoving, at the frozen delight in her hand. Tentatively, she explored the ice with the tip of her tongue, and smiled.

I found myself smiling with her. I cocked my head and looked at the serious young face of Cephus Smith.

"Do you feel optimistic about your future in Mississippi?" I asked.

"No. No, I don't," he said somberly.

"Oh? Well, do you think you'll see radical changes in your life-time?" I persisted.

The solemn voice never changed. "I know I will. There will be changes, but I can't yet see how the changes will be."

I grinned at him. "I wish you luck, Cephus!"

"I have luck," he said.

29

A gas station doubled at the local bus terminal. At ten o'clock at night it shone like a bright neon island in the shadowed streets of Cleveland, Mississippi. An empty lot adjoining the station acted as parking space for the cars of those about to depart or arrive. Now it was jammed with cars haphazardly idling on the cindered surface, awaiting the Trailways bus going north to Memphis. Two marines and a sailor had piled their duffles and sea bags on the hood of a Ford. They lounged on the fenders, drinking steadily from cartons of beer cans they fished from the back seat. They never paused as I edged the Chevvy past them, seeking a space where we could wait. They simply turned and watched.

Linda was leaving Ruleville for a two-week holiday at home, and I had driven her to Cleveland to meet the bus. As she climbed out and made her way through the tangle of cars to the gas station office, she was followed by a stream of Negro teen-agers who had come to see her off. Their laughter and high spirits wound like a scarlet ribbon through the lot. By the time they made it to the office door, every eye was on the party. As I locked my car, I sensed the tension and hurried with Linda's bag to join them. She had purchased her ticket and stood now against the white-washed side of the station, surrounded by the good-natured Negro kids. Her laughter peeled above the joshing banter, and I marveled at her total unself-consciousness. The blue-white arc lights of the station framed the group. Anywhere in America, I thought it would have drawn attention. Linda was pretty. She looked like what she was, a refined white girl from a good family in Winnetka, Illinois. In Mississippi, surrounded by Negro boys and girls who treated her as one of their own, her impeccable manners and natural warmth was an affront to every white in the station. I swung the suitcase onto the raised walk next to Linda and peered anxiously down the highway for signs of the Trailways bus. A car pulled into the crowded lot and parked alongside my Chevvy. Cephus Smith never turned from our group, but he said very quietly, "Don't get boxed in. You may want to leave quick." I ran my eyes casually over the lot, reading the signs. Almost every car held whites. The sailor and marines had been joined by two stocky men in sport shirts from an adjoining car. Like their girlfriends who stared through the windshield, their eyes were fastened on our little group.

"Cephus," I said, "I'm going to order gas and then park opposite the pump. Soon as Linda is on the bus, get the kids in the car." Averting the challenging stares, I crossed the lot and climbed into the Chevvy. Easing the car out, I moved alongside the pump, filled the tank, and parked it, motor running, on the edge of the blacktop. As I rejoined Linda, the bus sounded its horn and rolled majestically into the station. Car doors swung open, and people surged toward the bus. Linda, laughing, climbed aboard the bus, waving and calling gay good-bys to her friends from Ruleville. I took the bag from Cephus and mounted the steps behind her. As I swung the suitcase into the luggage rack above her seat, Linda's face was serious and pale. "I hope you don't have trouble," she said softly.

"No trouble, Linda," I said. I nodded at the Chevvy at the edge of

Linda Davis, Winnetka, Illinois; Oberlin College; Ruleville, Mississippi.

the drive. Cephus and the others were already in the car. I smiled. "Have a good trip home!"

I crossed swiftly to the car. We rolled from the station and headed for Ruleville as the line of passengers were still slowly mounting the steps to the bus.

The night before, we had sat late in the yard of the Community Center, talking quietly of the past year. I sensed that Linda welcomed my questions. Perhaps they enabled her to recognize what she had come to believe in a year. Perhaps they merely armed her for the ordeal of questioning that awaited her back in Illinois. At any rate, I found the evening a delight. And I felt, by its end, that I had come to know better a rare and special person.

"You've been here a year," I said. "Why do you want to return to Ruleville?"

"Oh," she replied, "it's for *me*. It's *my* need. Having been here has given me the courage to say that. Yes. I'm down here for myself. That's why I'm down here." She stirred in the darkness. Her voice had a soft piping quality, hushed—a little breathless. "I don't want to get into something mystical. It's not a mystical kind of thing that we're doing. We're organizing along political lines, trying to give people political power. So I don't want anyone to think I've got my head in the clouds."

"I know what you've contributed to this community, Linda," I said. "I've heard it from Mrs. Hamer. From Mac, from Mrs. Williams. I'm certain no one here thinks you have your head in the clouds."

She was still, and there was a catch in her voice when she spoke again. "Just who is contributing to whom is the question. I feel guilty sometimes—I really feel guilty. To the point where I wonder: 'Jesus! Am I really doing my work? What *am* I doing down here? Accomplishing?' It makes me feel kind of panicky sometimes. What am I doing to help people?"

The Delta spread like an endless velvet plain in the darkness, the sky alive with stars that were closer somehow than in Illinois. This girl-child, not yet twenty-one, so far from Winnetka—a fall, a winter, a spring away from Oberlin College, and still the questioning. "Am I down here so much for my own sake that it's wrong?" I was silent. There were no answers to be given by someone else. Each searched his heart and made his own equations.

"Maybe," she said, "I'm not in a position to judge. But when I talked to Mrs. Hamer about it—quite honestly—and tried to get beyond 'we love every white person who comes down here to help,' she seemed to feel that there really has been some contribution." There was a searching simplicity, a stubborn refusal to adorn her role that touched and moved me.

Linda Davis leads a modern dance group at the Freedom School.

"I've thought that if my being here with Mrs. Hamer ... our talks together, our friendship ... has helped her to keep going, then maybe *that* was my contribution." She hesitated. "Maybe I've helped a few people like that—maybe the McDonalds...." Linda stopped, and a small warm laugh bubbled in the darkness. "I was just thinking how I've 'helped' Mr. and Mrs. McDonald! I've worried them sick!" Her voice melted with the affection she felt for the aged couple. "When I was arrested the second time in Drew last spring, the whole community knew about it immediately because so many Ruleville people were up there with me. Poor Mr. McDonald! When he heard that I had been arrested, he had a relapse with his bad heart. When my father came down last winter to visit me, he stayed with the McDonalds. As fathers will do, he said to 'Mr. Mac' when he left: 'You see after Linda and take care of her for me.' Well, you know 'Mr. Mac.' He took this to the bottom of his heart, and when he heard I was in jail, he felt he had let my father down!" She shook her head mournfully. "Then some lady came into the quarter, swearing she had seen my car somewhere in a ditch between here and Cleveland. So who gets into his truck and trudges off into the night searching for me? Mr. McDonald. I've been some help!" The voice trailed off into the darkness.

"Maybe you'll be pleased to know that McLaurin thinks you're doing a real job here, Linda," I said. She nodded, but didn't respond. "I think the reason you feel guilty is that you're not functioning in Mississippi at all in the way you imagined you would when you were back at Oberlin."

"Oh," she exclaimed, "that's so true! It's funny. I go back North and friends say, 'What do you *do?*' And I don't know what to say! 'Well,' I start lamely, 'there's this community, see...!'" She broke off giggling. "It's *awful* trying to explain to people who work from nine to five what I do! I start to feel guilty that I don't put in a full eight-hour day! And then I figure, 'Hell, I don't get paid that much, anyway!'" She hooted with unrestrained laughter. "No one," she gasped, "would work for these wages!"

Linda's art class.

The joy that lurked just beneath the surface of Linda spilled into the yard—the tenderness she felt for people, her pleasure in the daily round of living, her ceaseless wonder at discovery of new facets of herself and her world.

"How much do you get paid by Snick as a staff person?" I asked.

"Ten dollars a week. When we get paid!" she laughed. "My parents used to supplement my pay, but then I learned some new things about money. Do you know that the middle-class value of 'having something in reserve' doesn't exist down here?"

"Maybe because there's no middle class in Ruleville!" I answered. She chuckled. "Maybe. Anyhow, it's become kind of a game with me, seeing how fast I can get rid of money! I've found you can go around absolutely broke ... and keep on living! You share when you have a little money, and when you're broke, someone else shares who has a little."

"Have your political ideas changed too, Linda?"

"I think I'm very naïve, politically, Tracy. More naïve now in some respects than I was when I came down. I'm less willing to compromise than I was before. Being here has given me such new ideas to consider! New ways of thinking, of listening, of letting other people talk—letting ideas come forth! I don't think our political system today encourages that enough. But I get so frustrated at times! I get caught between the pragmatic and the idealistic—between Laurence Guyot, the head of the Freedom Democratic party, and Bob Moses. It's a fine thing, all this political education and participation down here. But we're not electing anybody, either!"

She took a deep breath and plunged on. "And then there's my dad, who I have great respect for as a man of principle. He's very politically oriented and really believes in the workability of our institutions. So I have all sorts of questions in my mind: like the role of this kind of grassroots political organizing versus one significant person in a significant position who could bring a factory to this town!"

Lights from an approaching car silhouetted her fine profile that was saved from conventional prettiness by a slightly stubborn chin. Her eyes in the yellow light looked shadowed and introspective. "At this point," she said, "I'm not going to knock out any approach that can help bring change down here."

The car stopped beside the center. Cephus Smith and Charles McLaurin climbed out and waved a greeting as they went inside. They were preparing for the arrival of the summer volunteers who were expected the next week.

"It's a rare thing," I said, "to see Mac over here so late at night. I remember last summer that there was almost no social contact with him in the evening. He wasn't one of the boys you sat around drinking beers with." He kept his distance and I know it was a deliberate choice he made. It helped retain an aura of leadership when he was here.

Linda said: "He's right. He's always operated that way in this community—except on one disastrous occasion!" She started to laugh. "I could have killed him! Two months ago he came to a mass meeting stone drunk!" The recollection convulsed her, and she rocked with laughter. "*Crazy!* He sat there in the corner of Williams Chapel, calling out verses to 'This Little Light of Mine.' 'Go tell the Mayor now—that I'm gonna let it shine!' 'Go tell Mr. Charlie now—that I'm gonna let it shine!' 'Go tell all the Delta now—that I'm gonna let it shine!'"

She stopped, struggling for breath, trying vainly to contain her mirth. "He'd yell out verse after verse after verse. Everyone wanted to stop, but Mac kept singing out: 'Go tell Mississippi now' and everyone wanted to match Mac to the very end!" She wiped her streaming eyes. "He had them singing 'This Little Light of Mine' for *fifteen* minutes straight!" She dissolved in laughter. "I finally couldn't keep a straight face and I walked outside. I never laughed so hard! When I came back in the hall he started to talk. And he talked for *one hour and a half!*" She sighed, laughter and admiration echoing in her throat. "I was all set the next day to hear criticism from some of the ladies in the community—but, no! Mrs. Williams came up to me and said, 'Wasn't that McLaurin great?' And Mrs. Ruby Davis thought 'it was a *fine* talk!' I told Mac right then I'd never worry about him again!" Her silver laughter filled the yard. It seemed to speak of all the youth and promise that had come into this strange corner of America. I reached out in the darkness and touched her hand. "Linda," I said, "in case I never have a chance to say it again, thank you."

30

The Executive Committee of the Mississippi Freedom Democratic party in the county was to meet in Sunflower, and I stopped to pick up McLaurin at Amzie Moore's house. Since their marriage, Mac and Gloria had lived in the comfortable home with Amzie. Gloria trailed behind as Mac moved rapidly across the yard to the car. She looked lovely and young, younger than her nineteen years. Her brown skin was glowing against the turquoise cotton, and her hair was brushed and lustrous in the dim twilight. She was the oldest child in a large family, and from an early age had been a responsible partner to her mother in raising her brothers and sisters. Even now, almost a year after her marriage, she was on the way to her mother's home to care for the youngest children during the evening. McLaurin's insistence on keeping his political and his private lives separate had kept Gloria a stranger to the McLaurin we knew in Ruleville. Some in the Movement had assumed he had done it out of concern for Gloria's safety, and they respected his desires in the matter. Gloria privately fretted at being denied access to all of Mac's activities, but contented herself during the summer by assisting her mother. Once it was fall, she and Mac would be sharing college again. To her it was a great joy, and her aspirations for becoming a teacher were at last being realized.

As she climbed from the car in front of her mother's home, I was struck by the contrast between her and her husband. Gloria radiated warmth. She was known to be a gay and loyal friend. A determined desire for a better life than her family had known moved her to pursue college, plan a home, and establish a pattern of living that would allow for graciousness, however modest. She had fallen in love with this cool, complicated, and strangely passionate man. Often, now, she despaired that her husband would ever accept a predictable regimen.

Mac's scorn for her middle-class aspirations was boundless. "Gloria's friends meet at each other's homes—in turn! They eat stuffed celery and mix all kinds of fancy drinks that are too sweet." He had snorted his disdain. "Gloria," he observed despondently, "would like me to have an eight-hour-a-day job. I told her I don't want one. I'm going to be too busy in politics to get trapped in that kind of a job." With a voice that somehow missed the certainty he intended, he said, "I think she's slowly getting used to the idea."

I had looked forward to the drive with McLaurin. I found the time with him rewarding. Though he rarely initiated conversation, I found him completely lacking in reticence when asked a question. There was an amalgam of frankness and humor that was completely his own. I found myself insatiably curious about Mississippi, and he proved to be a fine Baedecker as I explored the political landscape.

"Is COFO dead, Mac?" I asked.

"Yes," he said promptly. "It was born a purpose in Mississippi, and the purpose has been served. It broke the boundaries—got things started. Now there's the Freedom Democratic party." His voice became thoughtful. "I think in the same way Snick will be through in Mississippi, too. And it isn't just because the original Snick leaders are disappearing. It's because they've done their job well. The leaders now are coming locally—from the towns and the cities. That's what Snick was set up to accomplish." He nodded his head vigorously. "And now those local leaders will act through the Mississippi Freedom Democratic party."

"Is the MFDP for real, Mac?" I asked.

"It's for real." The voice was quiet and confident. "With the 'poverty program' and the new 'Voting Rights Bill,' the MFDP can become a real force down here. It can help bring power to colored and poor white voters who have always been cheated by the power structure in Mississippi. But it can only do it if it stays clear of the old middle-class Negro leadership. Those folks are out of touch with most of the people. The MFDP leaders they have now, like Mrs. Hamer and Lawrence Guyot, are good and

they're tough. Mrs. Hamer is important, because she is like so many Negroes here. She's a day laborer, a sharecropper, up from the plantation. She speaks what they would say if they could. The country has said that an educational background is the whole basis for success. Yet all of a sudden, here's this lady from the backwoods who is saying things that educated people ought to have said but haven't said. She makes those people feel there must be others. With people like Mrs. Hamer, the MFDP can shake up this state."

The light was fading over the fields, and I relished the sweet stillness of dusk in the Delta. I turned on my parking lights. They were hardly necessary, for Route 41 never turned in its flight south. The air was cool and gentle after the sodden heat of the afternoon. We rode for several moments in silence. Lights began to wink on in the sharecroppers' cabins as we slipped swiftly down the highway. The small shacks were framed against the last light, looking like forlorn boats in the great expanse of fields. "We don't have farms like this up home," I said. "These just go on and on, for thousands of acres sometimes. You know, Mac, when I talked with two plantation owners earlier this week, they were genuinely worried about radical change. They're afraid that with the Negroes' new political power, tax reforms will be passed that will break up their large landholdings. Do you think that's likely to happen?"

I stole a look at McLaurin. His face was turned toward the fields. The pale light from the dashboard defined the thick chest and shoulders, but the face was just a darker blur against the night sky. He continued to stare at the darkening landscape as he answered. "I think it probably will. The big landowners with thousands of acres of land really control all the wealth of these little communities. The towns are built around the plantations and they depend completely on them. The owners have everything; the land, the tools, and the capital. Most Negroes own nothing but their labor.

If they start to vote, certainly they're going to vote to tax the Man. It'll only be right if they do. The Man has always gotten his land for little or nothing, while the Negro pays high taxes on every dollar he makes." He paused and turned to stare at the road that raced away from the beams of light. "And you know he doesn't make many dollars here in the Delta. So I can see it happening. I guess historically it's happened that way before."

"I suppose that possibility is at the heart of much of the resistance in Mississippi," I said. "Do you expect much harassment this summer?"

"Maybe." He brushed his knuckles along his chin as he weighed his answer. "Maybe some. I think there won't be as much trouble about the vote as there would be if we were going to spend our time testing public accommodations. Even the most hardened segregationist is likely to say now: 'Well, I'm not against people *voting*.' But if we really get large numbers of Negroes registered, then you may find some violence."

"From whom?" I asked. "The police?"

"No, I don't think so. I think we saw the end of most of the official harassment last summer. I think now the police are going to at least *act* as if they want to help, rather than be the ones to start the trouble. Trouble will come from the Klan and the self-appointed vigilante groups who have always had the law on their side. Now, when the voting registration tests are gone and the police start administering the new law impartially, they're going to say: 'There's nothing to do now but handle it ourselves.'" He lapsed into silence.

The first lights of Sunflower clustered near the railroad tracks that crossed the highway. I turned and drove past the desolate storage sheds that edged the tracks. The dirty streets smelled of diesel oil and manure, and the shacks that lined the road were naked of paint. I wheeled the car slowly around ragged Negro children who scattered as we moved into the badly lit heart of Sunflower. When we found the meeting place, I cut the engine and looked at McLaurin. "So what are you going to do when the vigilantes handle it themselves?"

He answered my question levelly. "I'm going to yell for the police," he said. "I'm going to force them to protect us or show up the breakdown in law enforcement in Sunflower County. And if that fails, I'm going to seek Federal protection."

I looked at the teeming roadway full of children and the gray rows of hopeless houses. How vulnerable it all looked! Sunflower County seemed at that moment as remote from Washington as Tanzania.

"What about *self*-protection, Mac? What about protecting yourselves by things like the 'Deacons for Defense'? The Deacons have been active in a few Negro communities in Louisiana, and some people think they've kept the vigilantes out of the Negro neighborhoods because the night riders know that the Deacons will shoot back."

McLaurin smiled. "I'm not condemning or condoning the Deacons.

People have the right to protect their homes when they're attacked. But I think our goal should be to make the police do what they're supposed to do. If they won't, and the Federal Government won't, then I can see where the Deacons would be needed." We walked up the steps to the screen door and McLaurin swung it open. "But *only* then," he said.

EPILOGUE: APRIL 2, 1966

As I close this book, Mississippi edges clumsily away from the legacy of race hatred that has crippled her children, black and white, and cruelly stunted her growth. Even at this late date, the moral resolve for new beginnings seems equivocal. She hesitates still to indict the murderers of Andy Goodman, James Chaney, and Mickey Schwerner. The killers of Herbert Lee and Medgar Evers walk her streets, unchallenged. An indecent inheritance of unexpiated crime and unspeakable violence has stained the state with guilt. Today, as "tent cities" of impoverished plantation castoffs rise in the Delta and Negroes throughout the state strain in frustration for their part of the "Great Society," the political powers meet in Jackson to consider seriously building a new "image" for Mississippi. In 1966 the Magnolia State still shrinks from the hard questions and the honest answers.

> *We been 'buked and we been scorned*
> *We been talked about sure as you're born*
> *But we'll never turn back.*

When the Delta Negro sings it, he cries. For him the song says it all. It's his sorrowing hymn, his anthem, and his exultant promise of victory. For the Mississippi Negro in this decade, promise of victory may be all he will know. But he will always remember that in 1964, for a brief hour, a thousand good people came to help him bear the cross. Their coming gave him strength and lifted his heart. And for their fellow man they lit a small beacon to challenge the darkness of their time.

A STRANGER AT THE GATES GALLERY

The following pages feature 26 additional drawings by Tracy Sugarman that were not included in the first edition of the book. All of Tracy's original *Stranger at the Gates* related art is housed at the Tougaloo College Civil Rights Collection, Mississippi Department of Archives and History in Jackson, Mississippi. http://mdah.state.ms.us/arrec/collection.php.

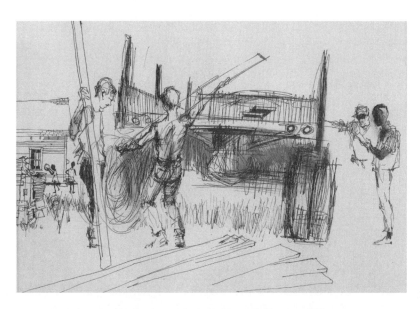

CONTRIBUTORS

Fannie Lou Hamer

Fannie Lou Hamer was born on October 6, 1917, in Montgomery County, Mississippi.

Hamer dedicated her life to the fight for civil rights, working for the Student Nonviolent Coordinating Committee for many years. During the course of her activist career, Hamer was threatened, arrested, beaten, and shot at. She was severely injured in 1963 in a Winona, Mississippi, jail.

In 1964, Hamer helped found the Mississippi Freedom Democratic Party, which was established in opposition to that state's all-white delegation being seated at the Democratic National Convention. She brought the civil rights struggle in Mississippi to the attention of the nation during a televised session at the convention. In addition to her political activism, Hamer worked to help the poor and families in need in her Mississippi community. She also founded organizations to increase business opportunities for minorities and to provide childcare and other family services. She helped establish the National Women's Political Caucus in 1971.

Hamer died of breast cancer in 1977. Andrew Young Jr., then a U.S. delegate to the United Nations, gave the eulogy at her funeral. He proclaimed that "None of us would be where we are today had she not been here then," according to the *New York Times*.

One of her most famous quotes is inscribed on her tombstone: "I am sick and tired of being sick and tired."

Congressman John Lewis

Often called "one of the most courageous persons the Civil Rights Movement ever produced," John Lewis has dedicated his life to protecting human rights, securing civil liberties, and building what he calls "The Beloved Community" in America. His dedication to the highest ethical standards and moral principles has won him the admiration of many of his colleagues on both sides of the aisle in the United States Congress.

He was born the son of sharecroppers on February 21, 1940, outside of Troy, Alabama. He grew up on his family's farm and attended segregated public schools in Pike County, Alabama. As a young boy, he was inspired by the activism surrounding the Montgomery Bus Boycott and the words of the Rev. Martin Luther King Jr., which he heard on radio broadcasts. In those pivotal moments, he made a decision to become a part of the Civil Rights Movement. Ever since then, he has remained at the vanguard of progressive social movements and the human rights struggle in the United States.

During the height of the Movement, from 1963 to 1966, Lewis was named Chairman of the Student Nonviolent Coordinating Committee (SNCC), which he helped form. SNCC was largely responsible for organizing student activism in the Movement, including sit-ins and other activities.

Despite more than 40 arrests, physical attacks and serious injuries, John Lewis remained a devoted advocate of the philosophy of nonviolence. After leaving SNCC in 1966, he continued his commitment to the Civil Rights Movement as Associate Director of the Field Foundation and his participation in the Southern Regional Council's voter registration programs. Lewis went on to become the Director of the Voter Education Project (VEP). Under his leadership, the VEP transformed the nation's political climate by adding nearly four million minorities to the voter rolls.

He was elected to Congress in November 1986 and has served as U.S. Representative of Georgia's Fifth Congressional District since then. He is Senior Chief Deputy Whip for the Democratic Party in leadership in the House, a member of the House Ways & Means Committee, a member of its Subcommittee on Income Security and Family Support, and Ranking Member of its Subcommittee on Oversight.

John Lewis is the recipient of numerous awards from eminent national and international institutions, including the highest civilian honor granted by President Barack Obama, the Medal of Freedom, the Lincoln Medal from the historic Ford's Theatre, the Golden Plate Award given by the Academy of Excellence, the Preservation Hero award given by the National Trust for Historic Preservation, the Capital Award of the National Council of La Raza, the Martin Luther King, Jr. Non-Violent Peace Prize, the President's Medal of Georgetown University, the NAACP Spingarn Medal, the National Education Association Martin Luther King Jr. Memorial Award, and the only John F. Kennedy "Profile in Courage Award" for Lifetime Achievement ever granted by the John F. Kennedy Library Foundation.

Charles McLaurin

Charles McLaurin, was born in Jackson, Mississippi, where he received his early education in the Jackson Public Schools. He attended Jackson State and Mississippi Valley State universities, studying political science and black history.

In 1961, McLaurin attended a meeting at the Masonic Temple in Jackson to see and hear a speech by Dr. Martin Luther King Jr. Inspired by Dr. King, the next day McLaurin joined the Student Nonviolent Coordinating Committee (SNCC) and took part in boycotts, sit-ins, picket demonstrations, and voter registration drives in Jackson, Mississippi.

In 1963, McLaurin served as campaign manager for Fannie Lou Hamer in her bid for Congress from the Second Congressional District. In 1964, McLaurin was a MFDP (Mississippi Freedom Democratic Party) delegate from the Delta to the National Democratic Party Convention in Atlantic City, New Jersey. McLaurin also directed the 1964 COFO (Congress of Federated Organizations) Freedom Summer Project in Sunflower County. During the Freedom Summer Project, McLaurin and Mrs. Hamer became close friends. They worked together on many social and political projects in Mississippi until her death in 1977. McLaurin and Tracy Sugarman met in 1963, worked together during Freedom Summer in 1964 and became lifelong friends.

McLaurin was arrested and jailed more than thirty times for his voter registration activities and for refusing to obey Jim Crow segregation laws in Mississippi.

McLaurin lives in Indianola, Mississippi.

Tracy Sugarman

Tracy Sugarman was born and raised in Syracuse, New York, and attended Syracuse University, where he studied art. During World War II, he was an ensign on an LST and participated in the D-Day invasion at Normandy in 1944.

After the war, he worked as an illustrator and moved to Westport, Connecticut, where he lived for the rest of his long life.

Sugarman's illustrations appeared in the pages of innumerable magazines and newspapers, including the *Saturday Evening Post, Ladies Home Journal, Colliers Magazine, Forbes,* and many others. He was a prolific illustrator of children's books and record album covers.

His painting "The Heroes of Nine-Eleven," is on permanent display in Washington, D.C., and his painting of the rollout of the Space Shuttle Columbia is part of NASA's pictorial history at Cape Kennedy.

The art he made during World War II was acquired by the Veterans History Project, a program of the American Folklife Center at the Library of Congress.

As a visual journalist, he created illustrations of conditions in the Rikers Island jail for the *New York Times* and was the only artist allowed to cover the Malcolm X trial, which he did for the *Saturday Evening Post.*

Sugarman wrote the memoir *My War: A Love Story in Letters and Drawings* based on his experiences in WWII. The civil rights movement of the 1960s inspired three more books, including *Stranger at the Gate* and *We Had Sneakers, They Had Guns: The Kids Who Fought for Civil Rights in Mississippi,* as well as his late-life novel, *Nobody Said Amen,* published by Prospecta Press and the Westport Public Library in 2012.

Tracy Sugarman passed away in January 2013.